Finding God's Will

Finding God's Will

Reaffirming the Sufficiency
of Scripture

Colin Hamer

ISBN 978–1–60899–878–4

Wipf & Stock
An imprint of Wipf and Stock Publishers
199 West 8th Avenue, Suite 3
Eugene, OR 97401
Web site: www.wipfandstock.com

For Elaine Ward,

who has held fast to the Word of life.

Contents

Preface

Can anything be more important in this life than knowing God's will—and doing it? Nonetheless, large numbers of Christians are confused about this very thing. Certainly in my lifetime, the Bible's teaching of a vital Christian experience has somehow become merged with secular ideas of spirituality and mysticism. As a consequence, the concept of the sufficiency of Scripture in the outworking of the Christian life has been left behind in many of our churches, both 'evangelical' and 'charismatic'.

To those who know about these things, this book may be seen as a defence of orthodox Reformed Christianity as outlined in various historic credal statements. But that was never my motivation. I have confined myself to the text of Scripture, and if my thesis finds affirmation in such statements, so be it.

To others, this book may be seen as a denial of the work of the Holy Spirit in a believer's life. For them, perhaps, no amount of protest by me will settle their minds—but, nonetheless, I do protest. I believe in an experiential Christian life in which my spirit witnesses with the Holy Spirit that I am a child of God. The same Holy Spirit dwells in me to motivate me to holiness. He interacts with my emotional life to strengthen me and to give me joy, peace, assurance and encouragement. These things are true for all genuine Christians.

My hope is that this book will reaffirm the sufficiency of Scripture and give Christians the confidence that in the Bible alone they will find all they need to know to please God in the conduct of their lives. I hope that believers will understand afresh the freedom and

responsibility this concept brings and be motivated to live the godly
life taught there.

Whatever our perspective on God's will, we surely all desire to
hear on that great Day, when every knee will bow, the blessed words
of our Saviour: 'Well done, good and faithful servant.'

That is my motivation for writing this book.

Colin Hamer
Warrington, 2010

Introduction

You believe your Bible. You accept that it is the final authority on all matters pertaining to your life of faith. God's voice is certainly and surely there on every page.

But is God's voice also heard elsewhere? Has he other ways of communicating with you? Does God speak to you, for example, in the events of your everyday life? You fail to get into university despite several attempts; is God telling you something? You are invited to a meeting and the preacher speaks movingly about being a missionary, something that has been on your mind; is God speaking to you? You have a dream that seems to confirm that you should go; is it from God? When, after much prayer about changing your job, somebody who knows nothing of this mentions a position that you feel would be just right for you, is this a message, a 'signpost' for your future life direction?

Is guidance to be found in miraculous spiritual gifts? Can we find affirmation of our life decisions in the signs and wonders of the apostolic age—a tongue or prophecy just for us? Is that sincere Christian friend right when he says that he has a word from God for you?

Many Christians would answer in the affirmative to some or all of these, and, as a consequence, make important life decisions on that basis. In a sense, this is perfectly understandable. All sincere believers want to do God's will. We do not want to miss an important task he has for us, an area of service for the Lord.

But contemporary evangelicalism has made the task of finding God's will more complex than it actually is by teaching a theology of guidance not found on the pages of Scripture.

The aim of this book, therefore, is to enable readers to see that God's will for their lives is found entirely in the Bible. And when they find it there and do it, they can make their lives count for God.

God's will defined

1. God's two wills

> The secret things belong to the LORD our God, but the things revealed belong to us and to our children for ever, that we may follow all the words of this law. (Deut. 29:29)

Before we can go directly to our subject, we need to do a bit of theology. Many Christians are not happy about this, preferring to leave theology to their pastors or elders—or, indeed, 'theologians'. This is a pity because theology in essence is about our understanding of God and his ways. What we believe about these matters has a profound impact on the way we think and behave. Many Christians are muddled about their theology of God's will and, as a consequence, muddle through their lives! I will cover this ground as simply as possible, then will move on in subsequent chapters to more practical issues.

Two wills

What do we mean when we talk of 'God's will'? Christians of all persuasions believe that God does as he chooses ('Our God is in heaven; he does whatever pleases him', Ps. 115:3). He wants something to happen, so it happens. He wanted our world to exist, so he spoke and it was there! This is not the same as saying that God can do anything; the Bible says that he cannot lie, and we know why this is: God is perfectly holy and does not want to lie, so he will never choose to lie. The problem arises when we see things happening in the world that are clearly not what God wants. He tells us in the Bible that he does not want to see murder, lies, theft and so on, but they are there for all to see. So is God not in control? Is he not able to stop these things? If that were true, God would not be God in any meaningful sense. Something would have to be more powerful than he, and perhaps that thing should then be called God!

We have quickly arrived at what theologians call the 'mystery of providence'. How is it that some things happen that we know from the Bible God does not 'want' to happen? If God controls all things, why is there evil at all?

Some have suggested that God is able to control everything but only chooses to do so some of the time; the rest of the time, he just lets things happen. He directs certain key events, and the rest he leaves be. To use the theological terminology, he 'decrees' some things, but not others. However, there is a problem: the Bible talks about God predetermining things in a way that would suggest he does control all things. If we take one example, the Bible tells us that God's church is made up of the 'elect', a group of people whom he has decided beforehand to save: 'For those God foreknew he also predestined to be conformed to the likeness of his Son, that he might be the firstborn among many brothers. And those he predestined, he also called; those he called, he also justified; those he justified, he also glorified' (Rom. 8:29–30).

Now if Liz Smith, yet to be born, is one of the elect, how can her conception, birth and rebirth to saving faith in Jesus Christ be effected if God is not directing every detail of life? These and many other details could be blown off-course at any moment! For example, imagine that a lorry mechanic fails to tighten the wheel nuts on the wheel of a large lorry; the lorry leaves the depot, loses its wheel on the motorway, crosses the carriageway and kills the grandfather of Liz Smith before even her father is conceived.

Some Christians have a problem with this attribute of God, which is often called the 'sovereignty' of God. They think that, if God controls everything, our existence is that of mere puppets acting out a macabre play in which all the lines spoken and actions performed are determined by the playwright. But this is importing human logic into a divine truth. And consider for a moment if the converse were true; the implications become frightening. No promise of Scripture would be secure. For example, Christ said that the gates of hell would not prevail against the church. In other words, the church is secure. Even if there were just one thing that God did not know, that one thing could cause the church to be lost—and make the promise invalid. If God knew that one thing but could not control it, the outcome might be the same. To say that God only knows and controls the 'big' things does not solve the problem; you are potentially left with those loose wheel nuts.

A further and more significant problem of trying to rationalize the mystery of providence is that the Bible tells us that God does decree some things that appear to involve evil acts, Calvary being a startling example. We know that Christ was betrayed by Judas, condemned by the Jews and executed by the Romans contrary to law and natural justice; but the Bible says of Christ's crucifixion: 'This man was handed over to you by God's set purpose and foreknowledge; and you, with the help of wicked men, put him to death by nailing him to the cross' (Acts 2:23). We have seen that God is holy and so cannot lie, but we must accept, in light of this verse, that he can decree certain things that involve evil actions without himself being tainted by that evil; this is one of the most fundamental mysteries of providence. God has a decretive, purposeful will which appears at times to contradict what he tells us he wants us to do (or not do). We can call the latter God's prescriptive will: things that God (like a heavenly doctor prescribing medicine) advises we do for our own good. An example of God's prescriptive will for Israel is the Ten Commandments.

So, at least to our human logic, God has two wills: a decreed will and a prescribed will. And to make things more puzzling, at times, as we have seen, they can appear to be at odds with each other, Calvary being just one example. Whether such a dichotomy exists in heaven we cannot know; the apparent paradox might just reflect a limitation of our human minds. Notwithstanding this, I believe it is helpful to see God's will in this way. His decreed or sovereign will is what actually happens; his prescribed, or 'normative', will (some might call it his 'moral' will) embraces the things he wants us to do. This concept, or 'key', becomes a powerful tool enabling us to unlock some apparent mysteries in Scripture. Whenever we read a verse of the Bible talking of God's will, we can now use this key to unravel its meaning.

Which will?

We have already seen that it was according to God's purpose, his decretive will, that Christ was put to death. But what about the prayer we know as the Lord's Prayer:

> Your kingdom come, your will be done on earth as it is in heaven. (Matt. 6:10)

Which will is being referred to here? Is Jesus asking us to pray that God's decretive will be done? This is unlikely because God's decretive will will be done anyway—nothing can stop it! No, surely Jesus is asking us to pray that God's prescriptive will be done on earth as in heaven. We are to pray that there should be no covetousness, adultery, theft, and so on.

> For this reason, since the day we heard about you, we have not stopped praying for you and asking God to fill you with the knowledge of his will through all spiritual wisdom and understanding. (Col. 1:9)

This must be God's prescriptive will. If the Colossians were full of the knowledge of God's decretive will, they would have been very full indeed. To know God's purposes throughout the universe even for a split second of time, let alone for eternity, would be beyond the capacity of any human mind to absorb. Paul was praying that the Colossians would come to know God's prescriptive will thoroughly.

> The Lord is not slow in keeping his promise, as some understand slowness. He is patient with you, not wanting anyone to perish, but everyone to come to repentance. (2 Peter 3:9)

Here we read that God is 'not wanting' (or, in the King James Version, 'not willing') anyone to perish. We have already seen that God has decreed who will be among the elect, so this verse must be speaking of God's prescriptive will. In other words, just as God does not want any evil committed, but it is, so he does not want any to perish, but they will.

For I have not hesitated to proclaim to you the whole will of God. (Acts 20:27)

This was Paul speaking to the Ephesian elders as he took leave of them. Again, this must of course refer to God's prescriptive will. Paul did not tell the elders everything that had ever happened and was going to happen. He was reminding them of how he had laboured among them, teaching the Christian faith.

Paul, called to be an apostle of Christ Jesus by the will of God, and our brother Sosthenes. (1 Cor. 1:1)

Here Paul was introducing himself to the Corinthian church. He was saying that God appointed him an apostle; it was something God did, so here we see God's decretive will.

Distinguishing which aspect of God's will the Bible is talking about in any given verse is vital for its correct interpretation.

How is God's will revealed?

God's prescriptive will, in which he tells us what is right or wrong and what we should or should not do, is revealed definitively in the Bible. Virtually all evangelicals accept this. They might disagree among themselves about what the Bible says; for example, some Christians believe that infant babies should be baptized, while others do not, but both groups agree that the answer is somewhere in the Bible.

Our conscience is also a guide but, although it is God-given, it can prove to be faulty. In some people, the conscience is damaged by mental illness, but even in healthy people the conscience can give wrong messages. Paul dealt with an example of this in 1 Corinthians 8: some Christians had a bad conscience about eating food that had been sacrificed to idols, but Paul told them that it was all right to eat this food.

One way to see God's decretive will is in creation. Part of the wonder of being a Christian is that we can look at any aspect of our amazing natural world and see God and what he willed into being:

The heavens declare the glory of God;
   the skies proclaim the work of his hands.
Day after day they pour forth speech;
   night after night they display knowledge.
There is no speech or language
   where their voice is not heard.
Their voice goes out into all the earth,
   their words to the ends of the world.
(Ps. 19:1–4)

All those stars, so many intriguing and strange creatures, the riot of colour, all that diversity: we can see from all this that our God is an amazing God and wanted us to be richly provided for materially—and intellectually, as we try to work it all out.

Another way to see God's decretive will is in the events of the past—they are, indeed, a perfect record of it. The day when I started work on this chapter, it was cloudy; as I write today, it is sunny. God decreed both. Anything that happens, he has decreed, even though, as we have seen, this does not mean that he necessarily approves of it. God has decreed that you read this book, or at least this sentence. But imagine that, to give yourself time to read it, you have decided to stay away from work and have phoned in to say you are ill. That is against God's prescriptive will.

The Bible tells us some parts of God's decretive will in advance. We have already mentioned one: that the church will be safe until the end of time. We are also told that Christ will return one day—a day we do not expect—to judge the living and the dead and take those who are his to be for ever with him. There are many such promises in Scripture which reveal something of God's decretive will. These promises were given to us by the prophets and apostles and recorded in the Bible.

Some Christians believe that there are prophets today and that future events can be predicted; it is claimed that these special people can give us a glimpse into the future. We will look at this in Part 3, where I trust that you will see that, apart from the past, which gives a perfect record of God's actions, and the Bible, which reveals elements of future events, God's decretive will remains secret.

This is what Deuteronomy 18:9–14 is saying:

> When you enter the land the LORD your God is giving you, do not learn to imitate the detestable ways of the nations there. Let no one be found among you who sacrifices his son or daughter in the fire, who practises divination or sorcery, interprets omens, engages in witchcraft, or casts spells, or who is a medium or spiritist or who consults the dead. Anyone who does these things is detestable to the LORD, and because of these detestable practices the LORD your God will drive out those nations before you. You must be blameless before the LORD your God. The nations you will dispossess listen to those who practise sorcery or divination. But as for you, the LORD your God has not permitted you to do so.

All fortune-telling that is trying to discern future events is forbidden by God. God's prescriptive will is for us all, but his decretive will is secret:

> The secret things belong to the LORD our God, but the things revealed belong to us and to our children for ever, that we may follow all the words of this law. (Deut. 29:29)

If any one verse encapsulates the thesis of this book, it is this one. Here God's Word clearly says that there are things God chooses not to reveal—they belong to him; on the other hand, in the law (the first five books of the Bible), many things are revealed, and they belong to us. In other words, within Scripture is recorded all that God requires of us, and it is all for our benefit, like our earthly doctor's prescribed medicine; the things God does not reveal, the secret things, we have to leave with him—we should not go looking for them.

God's decretive will is unknowable:

> Oh, the depth of the riches of the wisdom and knowledge of God!
>   How unsearchable his judgments,

and his paths beyond tracing out!
'Who has known the mind of the Lord?
   Or who has been his counsellor?'
(Rom. 11:33–34)

James explains that, although it is all right to plan, we cannot know the
future:

Now listen, you who say, 'Today or tomorrow we will go to this or
that city, spend a year there, carry on business and make money.' Why,
you do not even know what will happen tomorrow. What is your life?
You are a mist that appears for a little while and then vanishes. Instead,
you ought to say, 'If it is the Lord's will, we will live and do this or that.'
As it is, you boast and brag. All such boasting is evil. (James 4:13–16)

Supernatural revelation

So, unless God specifically tells us, we just do not know what the future
holds. We have to wait and see his decretive will unfold as time passes. This
normally happens through what are termed the 'laws of nature'. The
movements of planets, weather systems, earthquakes, births, deaths and
'accidents': studied by scientists, and largely given 'natural' explanations,
these are, in reality, simply the way God normally works. To achieve his
purposes, however, God sometimes steps into history and reveals himself
in an exceptional, miraculous way. The Bible records many such
incidents.

   At the beginning of time, God spoke in a miraculous way directly to
the key figures in history: Adam, Noah and Abraham, for example. In
Moses' day, when God's message to mankind began to be recorded in the
sacred Scriptures, he chose to speak through prophets, using miracles to
authenticate their message. Therefore, it is no surprise to find that the
miracles recorded in the Bible are not spread uniformly throughout
Israel's history; instead, they cluster round the time of Moses and Joshua,
and then again at the time of Elijah and Elisha, both these periods being
times of extensive new written revelation.

   And so we find that, in the New Testament, Christ confirmed his message with miraculous signs; more were performed by his hand than by any other prophet. Furthermore, we shall see that he authenticated his apostles by giving them miraculous powers.

God, however, did not restrict himself to recognized prophets; throughout both Testaments, various people, including unbelievers, received direct revelation from God. In the Old Testament, they included:

- Hagar (Gen. 16:13)
- Abimelech (Gen. 20:3)
- Rebekah (Gen. 25:23)
- Laban (Gen. 31:24)
- Pharaoh (Gen. 41:25)
- Miriam (Num. 12:4)
- Balaam and his donkey (Num. 22)
- Manoah and his wife (Judg. 13).

And in the New Testament:

- Zacharias (Luke 1:13)
- Mary (Luke 1:30)
- Joseph (Matt. 1:20; 2:13)
- The shepherds (Luke 2:10)
- The Magi (Matt. 2:12)
- Women at the tomb (Mark 16:6).

In addition, the book of Acts records what at first appear to be many examples of supernatural revelation. But in reality, during the first thirty years of the church's history covered by the book, there are fewer than twenty such incidents.[1] They are mainly confined to recognized apostles and prophets, although again there are exceptions, for example Cornelius, who was not a Christian or even Jewish (Acts 10:1–4).

So God does sometimes reveal his decreed will to men and women apart from through creation and the ordinary events of providence. But we can already see four things common to all these revelations:

- Each person received his or her revelation miraculously—usually through angels, visions or distinct verbal instructions.
- None heard an inner voice or received an 'impression' of God speaking.

- None was given a revelation of the mind of God concerning the organization of his or her personal life.
- All received their revelations at key moments in the history of God's revelation to mankind.

We will look at these aspects of supernatural revelation in Part 3, where I will contend that the Bible specifically teaches in both the Old and New Testaments that God will not continue to reveal himself in the same manner in the ongoing church age, as he clearly indicates in Hebrews:

> In the past God spoke to our forefathers through the prophets at many times and in various ways, but in these last days he has spoken to us by his Son, whom he appointed heir of all things, and through whom he made the universe. (Heb. 1:1–2)

But first, we will look at the source of much of the contemporary confusion in evangelicalism: the belief that God has a third will.

Notes

1. 8:26–29; 9:4; 9:10; 10:3; 10:11–16; 12:7–8; 13:2–4; 16:6; 16:7; 16:9; 18:9; 21:4; 21:11; 22:17–21; 23:11.

2. God's two wills— or is it three?

Therefore do not be foolish, but understand what the Lord's will is.
(Eph. 5:17)

A third will?

So far, we have seen that God has a decretive will and a prescriptive will. The former is largely secret; the latter is found in the Bible. In history, he has miraculously intervened in the lives of individuals to reveal elements of both his decreed and prescribed wills to achieve his redemptive purposes.

Today, many Christians say that they are looking for God's will for their lives. If they are looking for his prescribed will, we can immediately direct them to the Bible, and the problem is solved! There they will read that they are to love their neighbours as themselves, love God, not bear false witness and so on.

But, of course, this is not what most believers mean when they say this. They are usually at a crossroads in their lives, with decisions to make, and they do not know what to do. They want help from God; they want to know what God wants them to do.

Let's meet Ben, a young Christian man, and see if we can make sense of some of the life decisions he has to make in light of what we have learnt so far about God's will.

Ben sincerely wants to find God's will for his life. He would like to marry, and is fond of two young women in his church—Lydia and Alice—but he cannot decide which is 'the one'. They are both single, and both fine Christians. On his understanding of the Bible, Ben is free to marry either—but which one does God want for him? Ben does not want to get it wrong!

If we believe, as I have suggested above, that God's decretive will is all-embracing, the question is meaningless. God has decreed the outcome, and whether Ben chooses to propose to Lydia or Alice, it will be God's will as to whom he eventually marries. Ben is free to choose either. He is sure he is within God's prescriptive will (marriage is good—God recommends it!), and we know we cannot miss God's decretive will.

Because of the way in which Ben asks his question, we can see that, although he accepts that God has decreed certain things (for example, the security of the church), he believes that some other things are somewhere between God's decretive will and his prescriptive will. These other things are in a sort of no-man's-land between the two. Ben thinks that most of these things are immaterial to God: whether he has cereal or toast for breakfast, whether he wears brown shoes or black ones. But certain other things do matter, and, what is more, Ben believes that God has a view on them. In his mind, Lydia and Alice occupy this position. God has not unalterably decreed which one Ben should marry, neither does his prescribed will tell Ben specifically which one to choose; but, nonetheless, Ben believes that God's will lies with one of the young women, and he has to try to determine which one!

This is the nub of the problem. Many sincere Bible-believing Christians, those new to the faith as well as those who have been on the road for many years, believe that God has such a 'third way'. They believe that God controls and decrees certain 'big' things which work their way out in providence (Noah's flood, Calvary, the return of Christ) and that he has told us in the Bible what to believe and how to behave as Christians, but that between those two categories are many things on which God has a view but has not chosen to reveal it in Scripture. Various well-meaning Christians have shared with Ben different methods they have of finding this third way: they vary from interpreting the events of their lives as 'signposts' pointing the way to the correct decision; looking to how they feel about the matter to be decided and seeing in that an indication of God's will; simply 'taking it to the Lord in prayer'; or any combination of all three. We will look at these three methods in the next three chapters.

If this were not complication enough, there is another problem: there is no definitive list as to what occupies this middle ground between God's decretive and his prescriptive wills. For example, some days, Ben goes to work on the bus; other days, he goes in his car. How should he decide on any one day which to do? Should he 'take it to the Lord'? He has already worked out that, although some decisions seem very small, they nonetheless can have enormous consequences. If he decided to take the bus, but when crossing the road that morning to the bus stop was knocked down and killed, he would have made the biggest decision of his life without realizing it.

Why do so many Christians believe in this 'third way'? Especially when there is no agreement on what belongs there, and no agreed method (and certainly no biblical method) of finding it? There are probably many answers. Ever since we lost communion with God in Eden, we have had a deep psychological need to 'connect' with him in a meaningful way. We want to do as Adam did: walk and talk with God in the cool of the evening, and feel that he is there to direct us personally through the maze of decisions that life presents to us. And certain Bible verses, if taken out of context, might seem to suggest that God wants us to search out the life plan he has for us. Here is a selection from those that are often quoted:

> Show me your ways, O LORD,
>   teach me your paths;
> guide me in your truth and teach me,
>   for you are God my Saviour,
>   and my hope is in you all day long.
> (Ps. 25:4–5)

This appears to suggest personal guidance—but then in verses 7–10, David goes on to say:

> Remember not the sins of my youth
>   and my rebellious ways;
> according to your love remember me,

for you are good, O LORD.
Good and upright is the LORD;
    therefore he instructs sinners in his ways.
He guides the humble in what is right
    and teaches them his way.
All the ways of the LORD are loving and faithful
    for those who keep the demands of his covenant.

So the 'paths' and 'his ways' are found in the demands of the covenant.
David is asking for help to leave the sins of his youth and instead to fulfil
the demands of his God. In other words, David wants help to see clearly
God's prescriptive will as recorded in Scripture, and so live a holy life.

I will instruct you and teach you in the way you should go;
    I will counsel you and watch over you.
(Ps. 32:8)

Some commentaries suggest that this is God talking directly to David,
and see this as an example of direct divine guidance. But even if this is
God speaking, is he promising to give David specific guidance for his life
decisions? The context of the Psalm is almost certainly David's
repentance from his sin with Bathsheba and his subsequent restoration to
fellowship with God. Is it not more likely, then, that if this is God
speaking, he is saying that he will now direct David along a righteous,
sinless path? That seems to fit the context of the psalm. In any case, it must
be remembered that David was a prophet and that God did indeed speak
directly to him; the experience of God that a prophet has cannot always
be applied without qualification to every Christian.

Trust in the LORD with all your heart
    and lean not on your own understanding;
in all your ways acknowledge him,
    and he will make your paths straight.
(Prov. 3:5–6)

In the King James Version, 'make your paths straight' is rendered 'direct thy paths', lending weight to the view that God is going to guide us in individual life plans. Apart from the fact that the New International Version is considered by many to give a more accurate translation here, the immediate context, as well as the wider context in Proverbs, would suggest that it is talking about choosing the path of wisdom and godliness.

> Although the Lord gives you the bread of adversity and the water of affliction, your teachers will be hidden no more; with your own eyes you will see them. Whether you turn to the right or to the left, your ears will hear a voice behind you, saying, 'This is the way; walk in it.' (Isa. 30:20–21)

The phrase 'your teachers' is in some translations given as 'He, your Teacher' (e.g. the New American Standard Bible), as if it is the Holy Spirit who is referred to. Again, the New International Version gives the better translation of the text and fits the context better. It seems that these verses were written when the prophets were in hiding for fear of King Ahaz (the situation referred to in vv. 8–11). The promised blessing would be seen when Israel repented (v. 19) and the prophets would come out of hiding and teach Israel God's ways again. In other words, the passage is about literal eyes, ears and voices.

> 'For I know the plans I have for you,' declares the LORD, 'plans to prosper you and not to harm you, plans to give you hope and a future.' (Jer. 29:11)

The context clearly shows that God is speaking specifically to the Jewish exiles about the plans he has for them after the Babylonian captivity. Christians often claim this verse as a promise to themselves, but they take the verse out of context. Few Christians claim Jeremiah 18:11, a promise to Judah and those living in Jerusalem: 'This is what the LORD says: Look! I am preparing a disaster for you and devising a plan against you.'

Another Scripture often quoted out of context is Romans 12:1–2:

Therefore, I urge you, brothers, in view of God's mercy, to offer your
bodies as living sacrifices, holy and pleasing to God—this is your
spiritual act of worship. Do not conform any longer to the pattern of
this world, but be transformed by the renewing of your mind. Then
you will be able to test and approve what God's will is—his good,
pleasing and perfect will.

After the long doctrinal section of chapters 1–11, Paul turns his attention
in chapters 12–16 to the implications of these teachings. We are to renew
our minds in light of his teaching and live in a manner consistent with it.
So here we see again teaching about God's prescribed will; knowledge of
it should give rise to holy living.

   And Ephesians 5:15–17:

Be very careful, then, how you live—not as unwise but as wise,
making the most of every opportunity, because the days are evil.
Therefore do not be foolish, but understand what the Lord's will is.

Paul again makes it clear in the very next verses (vv. 18–20) that he is
talking about holiness—conforming our lives to the revealed prescribed
will of God: 'Do not get drunk on wine, which leads to debauchery.
Instead, be filled with the Spirit. Speak to one another with psalms, hymns
and spiritual songs. Sing and make music in your heart to the Lord, always
giving thanks to God the Father for everything, in the name of our Lord
Jesus Christ.'

   Perhaps for some, Ephesians 2:10 might give an impression that we
need to discover some specific work which God has planned for us to do:

For we are God's workmanship, created in Christ Jesus to do good
works, which God prepared in advance for us to do.

But there is no other verse which speaks of these good works forming a
predetermined life plan, or that tells how a believer should start looking
for it.

   These verses are just a small selection, but if we apply the understanding of God's will outlined here to any verse in the Bible that speaks of his will, we see that, when read in context, those verses show clearly that they are referring either to God's (usually secret) decretive will, or to his revealed, prescriptive will. I do not believe that there is a single verse in the Bible that says that a believer can ask God to reveal an individual life plan, or, indeed, that any verse exhorts a believer to look for such a plan.

Nonetheless, many books have been written and many sermons preached on guidance, often by eminent Christians, that assume such is to be found. But without a framework of understanding the nature of God's will, much of what is written or said is speculation and, in fact, can be quite harmful. Christians are often paralysed by looking for something that God chooses not to reveal.

That's enough theology for now—let's get back to the practical problem at hand! How can Ben make his life choices, and, in particular, choose between Lydia and Alice? I hope you can see straight away that, using the tools he has equipped himself with, he has a hopeless task. Why?

For three reasons:

1. As we have seen, the Bible nowhere indicates that there is such a third way—a will of God between his decretive and prescriptive wills.
2. What is more, no two Christians agree as to which things are in this middle category of things that need to be enquired about. Most who believe in a third way accept that the choice of marriage partner, employment, church and home are in there somewhere—but what about the car, the holiday, and which school the children should attend? Does God have a view on these things that he is waiting to be asked about?
3. What is worse, the Bible gives no mechanism for finding the answers. There is no 'guidance' teaching in the Bible for this third way, so, even if it exists, there are no means given in Scripture for finding it.

Let's stick with Ben through the next few chapters and see how he does. Basing our thoughts on our understanding of God's will, we will see whether we can make sense of some of his life events and the decisions he has to make.

God's will sought

3. God's will and providential signposts

His disciples asked him, 'Rabbi, who sinned, this man or his parents, that he was born blind?' (John 9:2)

Popping the question

The church weekend will soon be here and Ben thinks that it will provide an ideal opportunity for him to decide between Alice and Lydia. He has been listening to some advice from other Christians and they have told him that, if his heart is right, God will certainly guide him to the right girl. He has heard many speak of how God indicates his will through providential acts—the circumstances of our lives—and so gives clear signposts that take us along the paths he wants for us.

Friday arrives and, as Ben reaches the venue, he is both surprised and disappointed that Lydia is not there; she is ill and unable to come. But then he thinks, 'That's it! How could God be clearer?' He now looks forward to spending time with Alice over the weekend and, if it goes well, as he is sure it will, he will broach the subject of marriage with her.

But there are so many people on the weekend that he and Alice are split into different groups for seminars; even meals have two sittings, and Ben shares none with Alice. What is God saying now? Ben decides to consult Tom, one of the elders at his church.

Interpreting providences

Tom explains to Ben that many Christians look to interpret the events of their daily lives in this way—they use 'providential signposts'. They see in them messages from God. This is sometimes done on a national scale: a

hurricane or flood might be deemed to be the judgement of God on a
sinful nation. But, on the whole, the Bible speaks against making such
connections. Job, one of the oldest books of the Bible, is a book about
suffering, the nature of true faith and the mystery of providence. An
important lesson of the book is that Job's friends (his so-called
'comforters') got it wrong when they tried to tell Job why he was
suffering, even though they claimed to have had 'spiritual' revelation. In
Job 4:12–16, Eliphaz said,

> A word was secretly brought to me,
>   my ears caught a whisper of it.
> Amid disquieting dreams in the night,
>   when deep sleep falls on men,
> fear and trembling seized me
>   and made all my bones shake.
> A spirit glided past my face,
>   and the hair on my body stood on end.
> It stopped,
>   but I could not tell what it was.
> A form stood before my eyes,
>   and I heard a hushed voice.

But the 'comforters' were criticized by God for their explanations, as we
see, for example, in Job 42:7: 'After the LORD had said these things to Job,
he said to Eliphaz the Temanite, "I am angry with you and your two
friends, because you have not spoken of me what is right, as my servant
Job has."' In God's long reply to them, he gave no explanation of Job's
suffering; instead, he simply challenged Job and his friends to consider his
own sovereignty. For example, Job 38:1–5 says,

> Then the LORD answered Job out of the storm. He said:
> 'Who is this that darkens my counsel
>   with words without knowledge?
> Brace yourself like a man;
>   I will question you,

and you shall answer me.
Where were you when I laid the earth's foundation?
  Tell me, if you understand.
Who marked off its dimensions? Surely you know!
  Who stretched a measuring line across it?

It is impossible not to see in the tone of God's response that he disapproved of the interpretation of his sovereign acts.

Old Testament providential signposts

But Ben says that he is sure that the Old Testament teaches that some disasters were the judgements of God. What about Sodom and Gomorrah, for example, and that devastating swarm of locusts in Joel 2? The LORD described the latter as 'my great army'. Tom replies that, on such occasions, it was God who gave the commentary. But without such divine interpretation, how are we to judge?

Nonetheless, Ben considers that there were specific providential signposts in the Old Testament. In other words, he says, some things were interpreted as God's specific dealings, and taken as either guidance or judgement. Tom replies that care needs to be taken when looking back into Israel's history. God did guide that nation at different times and in different ways to achieve his purposes. In the desert wanderings, the Israelites had the fire by night and cloud by day to lead them (Exod. 13:21–22). Some battle tactics, it seems, were dictated by God, sometimes through providential signs (e.g. 1 Sam. 14:6–15). Also, there was the strange Urim and Thummin. These appear to have been stones on the breastplate of the high priest, which he wore when he went into the presence of God. By some means, he would use them to ascertain the will of God on any important matter affecting the nation (Exod. 28:30; Lev. 8:8; Num. 27:21; Neh. 7:65). But all this guidance related to the nation as a nation—not to individuals about their individual lives.

A wife for Isaac

But Ben persists and asks Tom to explain the incident in Genesis 24, when Abraham's servant was sent to look for a bride for Isaac. Tom agrees that this passage appears to confirm conventional guidance teaching for two reasons: firstly, because the guidance was specific for an individual; and secondly, because it involved interpreting a circumstantial providence:

> Then he [the servant] prayed, 'O LORD, God of my master Abraham, give me success today, and show kindness to my master Abraham. See, I am standing beside this spring, and the daughters of the townspeople are coming out to draw water. May it be that when I say to a girl, "Please let down your jar that I may have a drink," and she says, "Drink, and I'll water your camels too"—let her be the one you have chosen for your servant Isaac. By this I will know that you have shown kindness to my master.' (Gen. 24:12–14)

But, Tom explains, Isaac had to marry to fulfil God's promise to Abraham of a nation from his seed. Furthermore, God had specifically promised Abraham an angel to guide the servant to ensure that Isaac found the right wife (vv. 7,40). This passage is about God revealing his will to the prophet Abraham and giving guidance to that end via an angel to achieve his specific purposes for his nation Israel.

But we know that, today, God deals with his church, not the outward, physical nation of Israel. Christ transmitted his specific commands for the church to the apostles—and, says Tom, I do not believe that there are any such apostles today.

A fleece for Gideon
'What about the story of Gideon in Judges 6?' asks Ben. 'Many Christians talk about "putting out a fleece". They are undecided about a course of action—whether to do A or B—so they set up a sort of test as Gideon did."

Tom says that Gideon did indeed put out a fleece of wool and asked God to confirm by some unusual providences what he was telling him to do. But when we look at that story carefully, we see that Gideon had already been told by God what to do; he had had direct, clear, verbal revelation. The 'test' he decided on was to receive reassurance from God—a test with which God graciously complied. Tom suggests that it is difficult not to see Gideon as demonstrating a remarkable lack of faith, if not downright disobedience.

New Testament providential signposts

Ben asks Tom whether there are not similar incidents in the New Testament. Tom replies that Jesus appeared to reject the notion that we can interpret providence:

> His disciples asked him, 'Rabbi, who sinned, this man or his parents, that he was born blind?' 'Neither this man nor his parents sinned,' said Jesus, 'but this happened so that the work of God might be displayed in his life.' (John 9:2–3)

> Now there were some present at that time who told Jesus about the Galileans whose blood Pilate had mixed with their sacrifices. Jesus answered, 'Do you think that these Galileans were worse sinners than all the other Galileans because they suffered this way? I tell you, no! But unless you repent, you too will all perish. Or those eighteen who died when the tower in Siloam fell on them—do you think they were more guilty than all the others living in Jerusalem? I tell you, no! But unless you repent, you too will all perish.' (Luke 13:1–5)

Tom asks whether, if on these occasions Jesus did not look to give the reasons for seemingly arbitrary providences, should we? But despite this clear message of Scripture, many do make such deductions and are often swung from one conclusion to another as the circumstances are variously interpreted, or as events simply move on:

> When the islanders saw the snake hanging from his [Paul's] hand, they said to each other, 'This man must be a murderer; for though he escaped from the sea, Justice has not allowed him to live.' But Paul shook the snake off into the fire and suffered no ill effects. The people expected him to swell up or suddenly fall dead, but after waiting a long time and seeing nothing unusual happen to him, they changed their minds and said he was a god. (Acts 28:4–6)

Of course, certain sins do bring their own retribution. Too much alcohol, and you might get a hangover; sexual immorality can give rise to sexually transmitted diseases. Notwithstanding this, suffering should not be seen as the specific punishment of God on sin—although all suffering is a consequence of that first sinful disobedience of Adam in the Garden of Eden. The Bible gives no indication that other providences should be seen as carrying a message—in fact, rather the opposite, as we have seen from Christ's specific teaching.

Open doors

Ben asks what Tom thinks about open doors: surely they are signs from God?

'In what way?' asks Tom.

Ben replies that he considers an opportunity for gospel work that occurs as a result of a particular providence to be God's leading that such an opportunity should be taken; the 'open door' is a sign. Tom replies that it is true that most references to an 'open door' in the New Testament do refer to opportunities for gospel work, as in Acts 14:27, for example: 'On arriving there, they gathered the church together and reported all that God had done through them and how he had opened the door of faith to the Gentiles.'

Paul and Barnabas did use this opportunity to preach the gospel. But on another occasion, Paul ignored an open door: 'Now when I went to Troas to preach the gospel of Christ and found that the Lord had opened a door for me, I still had no peace of mind, because I did not find my brother Titus there. So I said good-bye to them and went on to Macedonia' (2 Cor. 2:12–13). So an open door is just that: it is not a message from God; it is an opportunity to serve him that we can take or not, as we choose.

God speaking to us personally in a verse or a passage

Ben asks whether there are not examples of God speaking to Christians by either showing them or bringing to their minds particular verses.

'Of course!' says Tom. 'God presses on our minds and consciences his teaching; that is why we should be storing his Word in our minds (Rom.

12:1–2). A praying Christian will ask God to bring Scripture to mind in this way, especially at a time of particular need.'

But Ben says that that is not what he is thinking of; some Christians are suddenly struck by a verse or passage of the Bible and consider that it therefore contains a message for them, outside the purpose of the original context. He has heard of a young Christian woman thinking of going to Bible college; one day, she picked up her Bible and, as it fell open, she saw the word 'cedar'—the very name of the college that was her favoured choice! She saw it as a sign from God. Tom replies that the Bible was never intended to be used in this way. It is not a book of wizard's spells from which the magic can be summoned. Ben replies that a lot of believers he knows think that the Bible speaks to them in this way.

Tom then asks Ben to consider another Christian, a young man who is being tempted into an immoral relationship with a married woman. His Bible falls open at the verses which speak of David's adultery with Bathsheba. Is that a sign for him to commit the sin? Ben thinks this suggestion is preposterous: no Christian would accept such a justification! When pressed by Tom as to why not, Ben replies that the context of those verses must be seen. It was a gross sin for David that had serious consequences, and he regretted it bitterly. So, Tom asks, if those verses should not be taken out of context, why should we as evangelicals take any other verses out of context and press them into uses to suit our particular purposes?

Tom tells Ben of the church he attended as a young Christian. They used to pass round a 'promise box' which contained verses of Scripture written on small pieces of paper, rolled up and pushed into a slot in the box. As they picked them out at random, they became God's promises to them for the day. Of course, in a sense, any promise of Scripture that applies to Christians is a promise for all Christians each day. But there is no significance in the providence of picking a particular one out of the box.

Casual providences

Ben then asks Tom, 'What we are to make of day-to-day (what we might call 'casual') providences?'

He relates how, when he first moved into the area he now lives in, he could not decide which church to attend. Just as he was discussing it with a friend, a leaflet advertising a local church was posted through his door. Was this a sign? Was God saying that this was the church he was to go to?

Tom replies that we see examples of casual providences in the Bible. The apostle Paul, when writing to Philemon and asking him to accept Onesimus back as a brother rather than as a slave, speculated that 'Perhaps the reason he was separated from you for a little while was that you might have him back for good—no longer as a slave, but better than a slave, as a dear brother' (Philem. 15–16). If the apostle Paul accepted that some events just happen and cannot be given a definitive interpretation, then so should we. But Ben points out that small events can have huge outcomes, so surely God must have a purpose in them, a purpose we can deduce? Tom agrees that casual providences can have disproportionate outcomes, and suggests that they follow through a hypothetical example:

One day, Janet was late for work; she ran for the bus but missed it. Travelling on the later bus, she met a friend she had not seen for some time; he was a young man from a church she used to go to. They got chatting, they arranged to meet, and within two years they were married, and soon three children followed.

Tom asks, 'Could Janet see the hand of God in the fact that she missed that bus? Of course! Did she know that morning that she was supposed to make herself late for work? No; that would be contrary to God's prescribed will. A Christian should be a good time-keeper; indeed, Janet had to apologize to her line manager when she did eventually arrive at work. Nonetheless, being late fulfilled God's decreed will for her life. Could Janet say that God brought her to her husband? Yes, she could. Would it then be right to say that it was God's leading for her to be late for that bus? No! Indeed, that would be dishonouring to God. It was not true; and God would never suggest a sinful act to any believer or unbeliever. From our perspective, it was a casual providence that God worked through to achieve his own purposes.'

'And what about the church leaflet?' asks Ben.

Tom says that the correct response should be, firstly, to see whether the

Bible has anything to say about choosing a church. If we look there, we will see that we are to attend church (Heb. 10:25), and that we should seek a church that teaches the apostles' doctrine (Acts 2:42). If there is more than one church that meets this requirement, we can ask others for help in deciding (Prov. 15:22), or even ask God directly for wisdom (James 1:5). The leaflet should have been read in the light of this knowledge; it was not a sign.

Tom tells Ben that, as a teenager, he applied to go to university but failed to gain a place; he had to try again the following year, when, rather strangely (as most people who knew the university admission system remarked), he got an unconditional offer. At that university, he was converted and met his future wife. He could see that there were a myriad of small providences that had brought him to this position. Was he, then, supposed to have been reading those 'signposts'? But he was not even a believer! When he did come to faith, did he then have a new responsibility to interpret the signposts? But there is no instruction in the Bible to do this, and no mechanism by which to achieve it. His new responsibility as a Christian was to get to know, and obey, God's prescribed will as revealed in Scripture.

Signs and superstitions

Tom continues: the interpretation of signs as omens is the stuff of pagan cultures and was endemic in medieval Roman Catholic Europe. Today, many primitive cultures are dominated by this approach. In Madagascar, a country Tom has frequently visited, one tribe might, for example, see dogs as an evil omen and consider them *fady*; yet another tribe will see them as a sign of blessing. Often the origin of the *fady* is unknown. It might simply be that, in the distant past, an important elder in the first tribe was bitten by a dog, and a member of the second tribe was in someway helped by one. This sort of thing should play no part in the Christian life; instead, the Christian is free from all superstition. What Paul said in another context surely applies here as well:

But now that you know God—or rather are known by God—how is it that you are turning back to those weak and miserable principles?

Do you wish to be enslaved by them all over again? You are observing special days and months and seasons and years! I fear for you, that somehow I have wasted my efforts on you. (Gal. 4:9–11)

Does God speak in any providence?

Ben asks Tom this question.

'Yes,' replies Tom. 'But not by secret, subliminal messages. Some events will dictate a life change. If we believe in God's decreed will, we must see these as coming from God. For example, if you have set your heart on being a military pilot, but then discover that you have been categorized as colour blind (as apparently at least one in six males are), your career choice is changed for you. But even here we must not try to read a 'message' into the situation. It was not necessarily wrong to have had the desire to be a pilot; it simply was not in God's decreed will. We have to leave the reasons with him.'

But what about Lydia?

This is Ben's last question, the one he has been working up to all along. Tom replies that the absence of Lydia at the church weekend should not be seen as a message from God; it just happened. If he is still keen on her, he should find another time to talk to her, and not be blown off-course by an unexplained, casual providence. God is not sending Ben coded messages.

4. God's will and our feelings

The Spirit himself testifies with our spirit that we are God's children. (Rom. 8:16)

Our feelings—a guide to life's decisions?

When Ben and Tom next meet, Ben's question is, 'If providential circumstances are not a guide for our lives, what about our feelings? What role should they have in our Christian lives?'

'The brief answer,' says Tom, 'is that they are pivotal.'

If we have had no emotional response to the Saviour we read and hear about in Scripture, Tom explains to Ben, it is unlikely that we are Christians at all. When unbelievers hear the gospel message of a holy God offended by sin, of the complete and unmerited forgiveness that Christ offers, of his unconditional love for men, women, boys and girls and the hope of heaven he offers, if they belong to Christ, they will go to him to receive the cleansing that his atoning blood affords. They will then know the joy of sins forgiven and come to love the Lord who died for them. Who would not be overjoyed and full of emotion about this? It was on the Emmaus road that the two disciples found their 'hearts burning' when Jesus explained how Scripture spoke of him. For all who have come to know Christ as their own Saviour, their spirits tell them it is so: 'The Spirit himself testifies with our spirit that we are God's children' (Rom. 8:16).

Furthermore, it is our love for the Saviour that motivates us throughout our earthly life to serve him, to honour him, to obey him. If we are motivated by anything else, we are like the older brother in the parable of the prodigal son, who saw his father as a harsh and demanding taskmaster (Luke 15:11–32). Surely no person who is devoid of devotional love for the heavenly Father truly belongs to Christ?

But it is when we see our feelings as a guide to finding God's supposed third way for our lives that the problems begin. The Lord describes himself as the believer's brother (Matt. 12:50) and Paul calls God 'our Father' (Rom. 1:7), but these family analogies can be pushed too far. Christ does not literally talk to us as a family member might. Unless God has spoken in Scripture, we just do not know what is in his mind:

> For who among men knows the thoughts of a man except the man's spirit within him? In the same way no one knows the thoughts of God except the Spirit of God. We have not received the spirit of the world but the Spirit who is from God, that we may understand what God has freely given us. This is what we speak, not in words taught us by human wisdom but in words taught by the Spirit, expressing spiritual truths in spiritual words. (1 Cor. 2:11–13)

Paul was saying that we do not know what God is thinking unless he reveals it. Who did he reveal his thoughts to? The apostles, who spoke as Christ promised, 'in words taught by the Spirit'. The context makes this clear: throughout this chapter, Paul was writing of the message the apostles had been given—not a message of earthly wisdom but one which 'God has revealed … to us by his Spirit' (v. 10). Certainly, the Bible never teaches that any aspect of our emotional life as a Christian is a messaging system telling us what God would have us do.

'So,' Ben asks, 'where does that leave our feelings?'

Tom replies that all good things come from heaven above ('Every good and perfect gift is from above, coming down from the Father of the heavenly lights, who does not change like shifting shadows', James 1:17); so any good emotion, such as love, joy or peace, comes from him. Because God showers good things on all people, believers and unbelievers alike, some have called this 'common grace'. All things good, right and true, all pure emotions, are from God—but they are not a road map for our future actions.

These emotions do not indicate what God wants us to do.

'Let me give a specific example,' says Tom. 'Perhaps you feel you should bake a cake for your neighbour who has been ill. That is good. But it is not a command to be obeyed. You are free not to bake the cake. Nonetheless you do, and the neighbour is thrilled and your friendship deepens. Eventually that neighbour comes to faith in Christ. This was all in God's plan: it was his decreed will and you played your part. But to say that you "felt led" to make the cake is using language that the Bible never uses. It implies that God was sending a hidden message with your desire to bake the cake.

'Perhaps you feel you should go and help on the door-greeting roster at church. This is a good thing; you are able to fulfil that duty, and the church is looking for extra help. The desire to help came from God—but it was not a message. God was not telling you to do it. If a feeling were a message, it would be possible to disobey it. But in the Christian life, you cannot disobey a feeling; you can only disobey Scripture.'

The leading of the Holy Spirit

Ben thinks that he has a lot to learn in all of this, and decides to attempt some more questions. 'What,' he asks Tom, 'does it mean to be led by the Holy Spirit?'

Tom replies that many Christians perceive someone who is 'led by the Spirit' to be more spiritual than a Christian who simply studies the Bible and puts it into practice. These Christians interpret their emotions as leadings of the Spirit and act on them. They often quote Romans 2:29, and certainly at first sight that verse seems to suggest that they might be right. There Paul seemed to contrast the 'written code' (Scripture) with the work of the Holy Spirit: 'No, a man is a Jew if he is one inwardly; and circumcision is circumcision of the heart, by the Spirit, not by the written code. Such a man's praise is not from men, but from God.' But the Holy Spirit is the author of the 'written code', the Bible (2 Peter 1:19–21). The passage is not contrasting the work of the Holy Spirit with the words of the Bible; Paul was saying that the Jews read their Scriptures and thought that, by following the precepts contained there, they would attain eternal life. But eternal life is given by God in response to repentance and faith, not because of any rule-keeping.

If we look at the places in the New Testament where expressions such

as 'led by the Spirit' are used (shown in italics below), we can quickly see
from their context what the phrases mean:

> Those who live according to the sinful nature have their minds set on
> what that nature desires; but those who live in accordance with the
> Spirit have their minds set on what the Spirit desires. The mind of
> sinful man is death, but the mind *controlled by the Spirit* is life and peace;
> the sinful mind is hostile to God. It does not submit to God's law, nor
> can it do so. Those controlled by the sinful nature cannot please God.
>
> You, however, are controlled not by the sinful nature but by the
> Spirit, if the Spirit of God lives in you. And if anyone does not have
> the Spirit of Christ, he does not belong to Christ. (Rom. 8:5–9)

And later in the same chapter:

> Therefore, brothers, we have an obligation—but it is not to the sinful
> nature, to live according to it. For if you live according to the sinful
> nature, you will die; but if by the Spirit you put to death the misdeeds
> of the body, you will live, because those who are *led by the Spirit of God*
> are sons of God. For you did not receive a spirit that makes you a slave
> again to fear, but you received the Spirit of sonship. And by him we
> cry, 'Abba, Father.' The Spirit himself testifies with our spirit that we
> are God's children. Now if we are children, then we are heirs—heirs
> of God and co-heirs with Christ, if indeed we share in his sufferings
> in order that we may also share in his glory. (Rom. 8:12–17)

And similarly in Galatians 5:

> So I say, live by the Spirit, and you will not gratify the desires of the
> sinful nature. For the sinful nature desires what is contrary to the
> Spirit, and the Spirit what is contrary to the sinful nature. They are in
> conflict with each other, so that you do not do what you want. But if
> you are *led by the Spirit*, you are not under law.
>
> The acts of the sinful nature are obvious: sexual immorality,
> impurity and debauchery; idolatry and witchcraft; hatred, discord,

jealousy, fits of rage, selfish ambition, dissensions, factions and envy; drunkenness, orgies, and the like. I warn you, as I did before, that those who live like this will not inherit the kingdom of God.

But the fruit of the Spirit is love, joy, peace, patience, kindness, goodness, faithfulness, gentleness and self-control. Against such things there is no law. Those who belong to Christ Jesus have crucified the sinful nature with its passions and desires. Since we *live by the Spirit*, let us *keep in step with the Spirit*. Let us not become conceited, provoking and envying each other. (Gal. 5:16–26)

A Christian controlled by, led by, living by, or in step with the Spirit is one who puts to death the deeds of the body, who leaves behind the sinful nature and instead lives according to his or her new nature to serve the living God. Paul is talking about holiness—the Holy Spirit motivating us to live lives according to God's prescriptive will, a will found in Scripture. In other words, in the lives of Christians, the Holy Spirit points them towards, and gives them the desire for, holy lives; in the lives of unbelievers, there is no such agency operating, apart from their own consciences and the pressures of the culture and laws of the society in which they happen to live.

In any case, the role of the Holy Spirit is never described in the New Testament as to give personal revelations to ordinary believers about God's decreed will regarding their individual life plans, which is what most people mean when they use the term 'led by the Spirit'. Rather, as the passages above clearly teach, the Holy Spirit brings to life the teaching of Scripture in believers' hearts and minds, and motivates them to follow God's precepts described there.

Acts 15

Ben asks next about Acts 15. He knows that, in the early days of the church, there was pressure on new converts to conform to the Old Testament Jewish regulations—particularly circumcision. The elders and apostles at Jerusalem came up with a decision on the matter and expressed it in a way that suggests to Ben that they had personal guidance from the Holy Spirit: 'It seemed good to the Holy Spirit and to us not to burden you with anything beyond the following requirements: You are to abstain from food sacrificed to idols, from blood, from the meat of strangled animals and from sexual immorality. You will do well to avoid these things' (Acts 15:28–29).[1]

Tom agrees that this at least appears to suggest that the church leaders on this occasion were supernaturally directed by the Holy Spirit to this decision. But he thinks a better explanation is that they were pointing out that the Holy Spirit had already made his will clear about the Gentiles ('It seemed good to the Holy Spirit') in Scripture and in the miraculous events of the early church. There was the salvation of the Gentiles (vv. 7–11), the miraculous confirmation of the ministry of Paul and Barnabas to them (v. 12), and the Scripture prophecy of their inclusion (vv. 15–18).

Tom says that it is, perhaps, helpful to see the Holy Spirit as a magnetic compass—a compass pointing the believer towards holiness. In contrast, some Christians see the Holy Spirit as a modern satellite navigation system for life's decisions, telling them to turn left in 100 metres, then second right, and so on—only the instructions are given not by an audible voice but through their own emotions.

Feelings and the Holy Spirit

Ben asks whether Tom thinks there is any connection between the Holy Spirit and our feelings. Tom answers with an emphatic 'yes'.

'Let us look,' he suggests, 'at a selection of verses.'

Then the church throughout Judea, Galilee and Samaria enjoyed a time of peace. It was strengthened; and encouraged by the Holy Spirit, it grew in numbers, living in the fear of the LORD. (Acts 9:31)

For the kingdom of God is not a matter of eating and drinking, but of righteousness, peace and joy in the Holy Spirit … (Rom. 14:17)

But the fruit of the Spirit is love, joy, peace, patience, kindness, goodness, faithfulness, gentleness and self-control. Against such things there is no law. (Gal. 5:22)

If you have any encouragement from being united with Christ, if any comfort from his love, if any fellowship with the Spirit, if any tenderness and compassion, then make my joy complete by being like-minded, having the same love, being one in spirit and purpose. (Phil. 2:1–2)

We see from these passages that the Holy Spirit dwells in us as believers and interacts with our emotional life to strengthen us, give us joy, peace, assurance, encouragement and so on—but not a life plan!

Choosing between Alice and Lydia

Ben then says that he is not sure, in light of all this, what role, if any, feelings should play in decision-making. Tom says that our feelings have a huge impact in decision-making, and rightly so. It is just that our feelings are not signals from God; they are not coded messages. Tom suspects that Ben is at last getting to the question he really wants to ask: whom should he ask to marry him?

Tom explains that Ben first needs to get clear about God's prescribed will in this matter: has God said anything in the Bible about choosing a wife? Ben concedes that there is probably quite a bit in there about it. Tom suggests that they take a look together.

Firstly, it is acceptable to be married or single (1 Cor. 7:1). But any potential wife must be a professing Christian (2 Cor. 6:14–16). As to what sort of woman Ben might choose, he can examine the virtues of a godly wife as outlined in Proverbs 31, and consider how Peter describes holy wives from the past (1 Peter 3:4–6). Furthermore, the clear picture of marriage in Ephesians and elsewhere is that of Christ and the church (Eph. 5:25–33).

In light of this, Tom suggests that Ben should ask himself whether he is prepared to behave like the Lord Jesus Christ to the woman he chooses: to show unconditional, committed love and servant leadership. Tom points out that it is right for him to consider which young woman would be most likely to be able to respond to the role Ben has to play for the picture of Christ and the church to be worked through in their married life. Ben is further told by Tom that if he simply likes Alice more than Lydia, that is good too. God really does allow us to choose things we like: 'God …

richly provides us with everything for our enjoyment' (1 Tim. 6:17). To
suggest that God always wants us to choose difficult or unpleasant things
is to be like the older brother in the parable of the prodigal son, who sees
his father as a difficult taskmaster. But Ben should not see his feelings for
Alice, for example, as a message from God. If these feelings were a
message, it would mean, in effect, that God would be telling him he must
marry Alice. In 1 Corinthians 7, where Paul dealt with many issues
concerning marriage and separation, Paul never once suggested that
believers might be guided by God to their choice of partner.

Ben has some misgivings; this approach seems too rational, too
straightforward, and he knows that many people in his church use the
language of 'the Lord's leading'. Indeed, one of his friends, a mature
Christian, has already told him that he will 'feel right' when he has made
'God's choice'. Ben feels good about Alice, so feels that he can safely
describe this as the Lord's leading. He tells all his friends and proposes to
Alice. She accepts, and they are happily married.

But as time passes, Ben begins to think that the language he used was
misleading. Although prevalent in evangelical churches, and thought by
many to be 'spiritual', the language of 'being led' often gives rise to the
idea that God 'speaks' in some way to the believer through his or her
feelings. Ben is now not so sure. On reflection, as he analyses his own
decision-making process, he realizes that he could have more accurately
said, 'I have asked Alice to be my wife because I am sure that I can love her,
at least to a measure, in the way that Christ loves the church. I am sure I
can be the sort of husband to her that the Bible speaks about. Also, based
on what I know of my Bible and what I have seen in her, I believe that she
would make a great Christian wife.'

But at the time, he, like many, was keen to be an accepted member of
his church and eager to be part of his peer group, so he used the language
that everybody else used.

The call to the ministry

Over time, Ben grows in his faith and preaches several times at his church;
many comment with approval. An older man in the church approaches
him and suggests that he should consider whether he is called to the

ministry. Another decision and another dilemma for Ben! Ben knows that the Lord sends preachers into the world:

> Then he [Jesus] said to his disciples, 'The harvest is plentiful but the workers are few. Ask the Lord of the harvest, therefore, to send out workers into his harvest field.' (Matt. 9:37–38)

> How, then, can they call on the one they have not believed in? And how can they believe in the one of whom they have not heard? And how can they hear without someone preaching to them? And how can they preach unless they are sent? As it is written, 'How beautiful are the feet of those who bring good news!' (Rom. 10:14–15)

And that the Holy Spirit appoints overseers (elders):

> Keep watch over yourselves and all the flock of which the Holy Spirit has made you overseers. Be shepherds of the church of God, which he bought with his own blood. (Acts 20:28)

And Jesus gives gifted men and women to the church:

> It was he [Jesus] who gave some to be apostles, some to be prophets, some to be evangelists, and some to be pastors and teachers, to prepare God's people for works of service, so that the body of Christ may be built up until we all reach unity in the faith and in the knowledge of the Son of God and become mature, attaining to the whole measure of the fulness of Christ. (Eph. 4:11–13)

The difficulty is, how do we know which men or women? Is there to be a mystical experience to confirm whom the Lord is calling?

Ben decides that it is time for a trip back to see Tom. Tom comments that this is a sensitive subject, and one that divides evangelicals—often unnecessarily, as sometimes the confusion is in the language, not the concept. We have already discovered that, when talking about God's will, different Christians can think they are talking about the same thing when in fact they are not, often mixing up the decretive and prescriptive wills of God with an imagined further third will.

Tom points out that, undoubtedly, Old Testament prophets were called directly by God to their ministry. Deuteronomy 18:20 says, 'But a prophet who presumes to speak in my name anything I have not commanded him to say, or a prophet who speaks in the name of other gods, must be put to death.' In other words, the prophet's words were to come directly from God. Obviously, no person could speak such words unless appointed by God to do so.

Similarly, the disciples, later to become apostles, were personally called by Christ and subsequently promised by him that they would receive power to speak in his name: 'But when he, the Spirit of truth, comes, he will guide you into all truth. He will not speak on his own; he will speak only what he hears, and he will tell you what is yet to come' (John 16:13).

In the New Testament, only on three occasions was anybody other than the disciples called by God to a ministry:

- Jesus met Saul on the Damascus road and commissioned him as an apostle (Acts 9).
- The Holy Spirit told the church at Antioch to set aside Barnabas and Saul for their missionary journey (Acts 13:2).
- Paul was called to Macedonia (Acts 16:9–10).

The concept of a mystical 'call'—some sort of 'inner voice'—as a prerequisite for anybody occupying any particular ministry or office in the church is totally absent from the New Testament. In each of the examples above, it was an ordinary, earthly voice that made the call (as when Christ called the disciples), or some sort of miraculous audible voice, or a vision.

Ben then asks whether he should be looking for a miraculous vision or voice of some sort, just as these people experienced. Tom suggests that he is rushing on too quickly! What is clearly taught in the New Testament is that the ongoing ministry of the church of Christ should be in the hands of elders, and a list of qualifications is given:

An elder must be blameless, the husband of but one wife, a man whose children believe and are not open to the charge of being wild and disobedient. Since an overseer is entrusted with God's work, he must be blameless—not overbearing, not quick-tempered, not given to drunkenness, not violent, not pursuing dishonest gain. Rather he must be hospitable, one who loves what is good, who is self-controlled, upright, holy and disciplined. He must hold firmly to the trustworthy message as it has been taught, so that he can encourage others by sound doctrine and refute those who oppose it. (Titus 1:6–9)

This is very similar to the list of qualifications given in 1 Timothy 3, except that there Paul adds 'able to teach', 'not a lover of money', 'not … a recent convert' and 'have a good reputation with outsiders'. So in God's person specification for an elder, there are seventeen requirements in Titus supplemented by four more in Timothy—twenty-one in all. And not one of them is that such a man is to experience a mystical 'call'.[2] On the other hand, we read in 1 Timothy: 'Here is a trustworthy saying: If anyone sets his heart on being an overseer [elder], he desires a noble task' (3:1).

Where does such a desire come from? We have seen that all good gifts come from above. God specifically prepares all his servants: he knits believers together in their mothers' wombs (Ps. 139:13), numbers the hairs on their heads (Matt. 10:30) and so orders their lives to accomplish his purposes through them (Rom. 8:28). So if a man has the twenty-one qualifications and the desire to be an elder, we know that all these things come from God. And if the outworking of providence means that a church recognizes these gifts, aptitudes and desires in a man, and asks him to serve as an elder, and he accepts, then we can know for sure that his appointment is of God. All these providences were part of God's decreed will. If as evangelicals we want to use the language of 'the call to the ministry' (although because of its prophetic overtones it would be better, perhaps, if it were avoided), we need to understand that we are talking of an individual's gifting and motivation, and recognition of that gifting by others, confirmed by the invitation of the church to serve in that capacity.

Any Christian should be able to see God's hand in such a providential combination of circumstances. But no secret messages. No mystical experiences. No hidden agendas. That is not God's way.

Ben sees the wisdom in what Tom has said. He carefully considers the qualifications in Titus and 1 Timothy, and, although he feels that he can live up to many, what is uppermost in his mind is that he has no desire to be an elder. So he feels free not to pursue it at this stage. He does not have to agonize for a long period, waiting to experience a mystical call. He is learning the same lesson again: that God deals with his people in straightforward ways, and that all Ben needs to know to be able to make effective, clear decisions is to be found in Scripture.

A lesson learned

However, it is not long before Ben and Alice go to hear a representative of a missionary society speak about his work in Africa. Both are really convicted by what they have heard. They feel certain that this is for them: they want to go as missionaries and use their lives to serve God in Africa. Between them, they have all the skills listed for eldership, and so think that they will qualify as suitable missionary material. And certainly they have a great desire for this work. After much prayer for wisdom, they consult several friends and the leadership of their own church, and then apply to the missionary society armed with glowing testimonials of their suitability for the role based on Titus 1 and 1 Timothy 3, only to learn that the one important thing they need is the one thing they lack. 'When did you receive your call? When did God speak to you?' they are asked.

Ben and Alice share their new-found understanding about God's calling and the role of feelings in the Christian life, but no amount of reasoning from Scripture will move the missionary society which, although well meaning, has in effect set aside God's Word for its own tradition. Ben and Alice are learning that their own understanding of Scripture on this matter is not shared by all.

So they go to see Tom. He does his best to encourage them; nonetheless, they cannot help but show their disappointment. Tom comments that, despite this setback, if God wants them in Africa, they will go there! He suggests that they renew their prayer efforts.

Ben says that they want to ask about that ...

Notes

1. The word translated 'sexual immorality' here is *porneia* and most likely refers to the Jewish regulations about avoiding marriage with close relatives.

2. **John McArthur** has defined mysticism as follows: 'Mysticism looks to truth internally, weighing feeling, intuition, and other internal sensations more heavily than objective, observable, external data ... Its source of truth is spontaneous feeling rather than objective fact, or sound biblical interpretation' (*Our Sufficiency in Christ* (Dallas: Word, 1998), p. 32).

5. God's will and prayer

The prayer of a righteous man is powerful and effective. (James 5:16)

Prayer changes things?

Ben says that he has been thinking carefully about what Tom has been saying over recent weeks. He has always been taught that prayer changes things, but now he wonders how this squares up with God's decreed will. Ben asks how, if God has decreed everything, prayer can change anything.

Tom replies that he knows that, as evangelicals, we like to say that prayer changes things, but does the Bible really teach it? And what do we mean when we say it? If prayer does indeed change God's decreed will, consider the ramifications. Imagine that, in the distant past, a church fellowship had prayed earnestly for a very sick child (Hannah) who was 'destined' to die; the prayers were answered and Hannah lived. What is more, she lived a long life, with many children and grandchildren. If we think that the prayers of those believers really changed the situation, none of Hannah's descendants were within God's decreed will.

Now we know that all those who love God were first loved by him before the creation of the world ('For he chose us in him before the creation of the world to be holy and blameless in his sight', Eph. 1:4), so can none of Hannah's descendants, who, seemingly, are not in God's plan, come to faith in Christ? Furthermore, could any of them inadvertently thwart God's purposes? In other words, could God be taken by surprise by any of their actions? Surely not. Otherwise, for example, just one of them, by his or her reckless driving, might kill the

grandfather of Liz Smith (our believer from Chapter 1) before her
father is conceived, just as the lorry with its loose wheel nuts might.
God would not be able to anticipate the actions of any of Hannah's
descendants because seemingly none of them would belong to his
decreed will! The concept of successfully praying for something that
was never in God's plan just does not stack up logically—or, more
importantly, theologically.

So what does prayer actually do?

Alice, not surprisingly, then asks what prayer actually does, and what role
prayer plays in finding God's direction for our lives. Tom replies that she
and Ben should do just a little more Bible study to consider the theology
of prayer before they try to answer those questions.

> [Jesus said] 'Therefore I tell you, whatever you ask for in prayer,
> believe that you have received it, and it will be yours' (Mark 11:24).

This promise must be considered in light of Jesus' teaching in Matthew 6,
where we are told to pray, 'your will be done' (v. 10). We have already seen
that Jesus was there referring to God's prescribed will. In other words, we
are to ask that there will be, for example, no theft or murder, just as there is
no theft or murder in heaven; that children will honour their parents; that
people will come to faith in Christ. It seems clear, then, that we should
not ask for anything in our prayers that is contrary to God's prescribed
will. We should not ask for somebody to be murdered or for some other
sinful thing to happen.

   Furthermore, we have already seen that everything that happens does
so because God decrees it. If this were not the case, there would be
something, or someone, more powerful than he.

> All the peoples of the earth
>   are regarded as nothing.
> He does as he pleases
>   with the powers of heaven
>   and the peoples of the earth.

No one can hold back his hand
   or say to him: 'What have you done?'
(Dan. 4:35).

Many Christians are happier saying that God decrees only some things and that other things (usually those things outside his prescribed will) he simply permits. Yet evangelicals believe that God, as Daniel says, is sovereign over all earthly and spiritual powers. If this means anything, it means that he could force all things to conform to his prescribed will if he so wished. So in practice, 'permission' amounts to a decree. Furthermore, the Bible certainly talks as if God does indeed predetermine all things:

In his heart a man plans his course,
   but the LORD determines his steps.
(Prov. 16:9).

One of you will say to me: 'Then why does God still blame us? For who resists his will?' But who are you, O man, to talk back to God? 'Shall what is formed say to him who formed it, "Why did you make me like this?"' Does not the potter have the right to make out of the same lump of clay some pottery for noble purposes and some for common use? (Rom. 9:19–22)

In light of this, it does appear to be meaningless to say that, in response to prayer, God will change his mind about his decreed will; we have established that the Bible teaches that everything that happens is what he has decreed, so the 'new' thing would be his decreed will!

Abraham

Ben asks Tom to consider the story of Abraham in Genesis 18. Tom agrees that this might be seen as an example of God changing his mind. We read of Abraham pleading with God to spare the immoral residents of Sodom. He appears to negotiate a change in what God intended. But we know that in several places the Bible uses the 'language of appearance'. In other words, the Bible speaks from a human perspective. For example, when it speaks of the sun moving through the heavens (e.g. Ps. 19:4–6), we know that this is not technically correct: the earth moves in relation to the sun. But we see no anomaly in this; we often use language in a similar way ourselves. Could it be that Genesis 18 is recording the story in a manner that makes it meaningful to us? God shows us in the account that if there had been just ten righteous people in Sodom, he is such a compassionate God that he would have saved the city. In any case, we cannot take this account at face value. God must have known how many righteous people were in Sodom. Even if some believers are tempted to reject God's omnipotence when considering the extent of his decreed will, few reject his omniscience. Jesus said, 'And when you pray, do not keep on babbling like pagans, for they think they will be heard because of their many words. Do not be like them, for your Father knows what you need before you ask him' (Matt. 6:7–8); and, 'Are not two sparrows sold for a penny? Yet not one of them will fall to the ground apart from the will of your Father. And even the very hairs of your head are all numbered' (Matt. 10:29–30).

Prayer: a mystery

Ben says that he can already see that prayer, like providence, is a mystery!

'Yes,' says Tom, 'and like the mystery of providence, no amount of semantics or philosophy can get round the problem. Those who hold to the view that the elect are saved solely by the work of Christ, on the whole, also passionately believe in the mysterious necessity of gospel preaching to bring the elect home. And so it can be seen with prayer: God will do his will, but he has chosen, in an equally mysterious way, to make our prayers instrumental to that end.'

Tom recalls that once, when he was a boy of seven or eight years old walking through his village, he saw a man up a ladder moving forward an hour the hands of the large clock outside the jewellers', to adjust it for British Summer Time. Somewhat alarmed, Tom told his mother that they had just lost an hour! No amount of explaining by her would settle his mind on this; eventually, she said, 'Just leave it—one day you will understand.'

Tom asks Ben and Alice to imagine the Bible as a clock—one that tells the time perfectly. It tells us what we need to know, but not how time works. Furthermore, if we open the back of the clock and delve into its mechanism, we will be no clearer as to what time it is. The clock face, like the Bible, is clear and tells us all we need to know. The mechanism is God's, and, in the end, we have to leave it to him. Maybe one day we will know, but for now we need to remember Ecclesiastes 11:5:

> As you do not know the path of the wind,
>   or how the body is formed in a mother's womb,
> so you cannot understand the work of God,
>   the Maker of all things.

What, then, can we pray for?

This is Alice's question, as she tries to keep the men on track with some practical answers. Tom replies, 'Lots of things! In fact, anything that the Word of God does not forbid.'

From a selection of prayers we find in the New Testament, Tom shows them that we can pray:

- for our persecutors (Matt. 5:43–44; Luke 6:28)
- for children (Matt. 19:13)
- for escape from judgement (Luke 21:36)
- for all Christians (1 Thes. 5:25; Heb. 13:18)
- that God's kingdom will come and his will be done (Matt. 6:10)
- that God will provide our daily needs (Matt. 6:11)
- for God's forgiveness as we forgive others (Matt. 6:12)
- that we will not be led into temptation, but delivered from evil (Matt. 6:13; Luke 22:40)
- for boldness in proclaiming the gospel and for God to do miracles in people's lives (Acts 4:29–31)
- for fearless preaching (Eph. 6:20)
- to be filled with the knowledge of God's will (Col. 1:9)
- for open doors for the gospel (Col. 4:3)
- that the Word of God may be honoured (2 Thes. 3:1)
- for deliverance from evil men (2 Thes. 3:2)
- for everyone, kings, authorities; and for peace, quiet, godliness, holiness (1 Tim. 2:1–2)

- for sinning Christians (1 John 5:16)
- that the love of Christians may increase (Phil. 1:9)
- for people to have good health (3 John 1–2)
- that we be strengthened (Eph. 3:16)
- for wisdom (James 1:5).

We must pray by faith for things of which God approves—things we know from the Bible he wants to happen—even if we do not understand the relationship between our prayers and God's secret, decretive will. Is the thing you want for yourself or someone else good, right and true? Then pray for it—and leave God's decreed will to him!

What about specific answers to prayer?

But Ben and Alice want a specific answer to a question: should they go to Africa as missionaries? Tom suggests that, if they look at the list of prayers above, they will see that prayers in the New Testament are not framed that way. In other words, in the New Testament, an ordinary believer does not pray, 'I do not know what to do: A or B; please tell me which.'

Jesus on the cross asked, 'My God, my God, why have you forsaken me?', but we know that he was quoting from Psalm 22. No answer is recorded as being received, and probably none was expected. It is more likely that the prayer was to draw our attention to that psalm and Christ's fulfilment of it, and to the depth of the suffering involved at Calvary.

On the other hand, Paul asked that the 'thorn in his side' (2 Cor. 12) be removed, and he did receive a specific reply: '… he [God] said to me: "My grace is sufficient for you, for my power is made perfect in weakness"' (v. 9). But we see that Paul did not say, 'I felt the Lord was saying to me …'; the reply he received appears to have been an audible, verbal communication. As we have noted, we cannot safely assume that the way God communicates with an apostle, or even his own Son, is necessarily the same for us. Many commentators and preachers fail to make this distinction. Tom tells Ben and Alice that the prophets and apostles did receive direct revelation from God, and he would contend that we do not.

'Once this is taken into account,' he says, 'I think you will be hard-pressed to find anywhere in the Bible an example of a prayer request about a life decision that received, or even expected, a specific answer. It is just not the Bible's teaching, no matter how ingrained this is in our evangelical thinking.'

Should we, then, ever expect an answer to prayer?

This is the obvious next question from Ben and Alice. Tom replies, 'Yes.' Prayers in the New Testament often do expect an answer, but the answer comes in the outworking of providence, not in a 'message'. For example, when writing to Philemon, Paul said, 'And one thing more: Prepare a guest room for me, because I hope to be restored to you in answer to your prayers' (Philem. 22). So if Paul arrived, Philemon could take it as an answer to prayer. And in 2 Corinthians, Paul suggested that an answer to the Corinthians' prayer might be his and Timothy's safe deliverance during their missionary journeys: 'He has delivered us from such a deadly peril, and he will deliver us. On him we have set our hope that he will continue to deliver us, as you help us by your prayers. Then many will give thanks on our behalf for the gracious favour granted us in answer to the prayers of many' (2 Cor. 1:10–11).

These are the sorts of prayers we read in the New Testament, and the sorts of answers expected. The answers did not come as messages, but in the outworking of providence.

What about the role of the Holy Spirit in prayer?

Doesn't the Bible teach that the Spirit will tell us what to pray for? This is the next question Alice asks. Tom says, 'Let's see what Paul says in his letter to the Romans.'

> In the same way, the Spirit helps us in our weakness. We do not know what we ought to pray for, but the Spirit himself intercedes for us with groans that words cannot express. And he who searches our hearts knows the mind of the Spirit, because the Spirit intercedes for the saints in accordance with God's will. (Rom. 8:26–27)

If we look carefully, we will see that the Holy Spirit does not reveal to us what we should pray for; instead, he hears our prayers and then intercedes on our behalf. The Holy Spirit does not send us messages or give us 'leadings'.

The dilemma

'But where does all this leave us?' ask Ben and Alice.

Tom says that we see from the list of prayers above that it is legitimate to pray for 'open doors' for the gospel. In other words, we can pray that there will be opportunities for gospel preaching. This is not a surprise; we know that the New Testament urges us all to speak of the gospel. So it is perfectly all right for Ben and Alice to ask God to provide an open door for them to go to Africa.

'But how will we know if we *are* to go?' they ask. They have been advised by a retired missionary (Martin) in their own church to pray; he said, 'If the Lord is in it, be earnest in prayer and he will show you.' But Ben asks how they will know whether 'the Lord is in it'? Ben thinks that Martin's comment, although intended to be helpful, actually is not.

Tom asks why not.

'Firstly,' replies Ben, 'Martin gave no mechanism for us by which we could know the answer to our request; and in any case, if the answer is "no", does that mean that the Lord is not in it? That we were mistaken in our desire to be missionaries in Africa? Perhaps there is then the suggestion that our ambitions were not "godly"—they were something else. But we know that to serve God in the way we wish is within God's prescribed will. So we surely cannot be wrong in our desire.'

Tom agrees, but this is not the same as saying that going to Africa is in God's decreed will. Many things are 'right' but not what God has determined.

Is there no way forward for us?

This is the plea of Ben and Alice: 'Is there no specific thing we can ask for?'

'Yes,' replies Tom. In fact, there are many:
- They can ask God to fill them with the knowledge of his will (Col. 1:9), so that they are able to bring to mind the Scripture principles relevant to the many decisions that lie ahead of them.
- They should pray for wisdom (James 1:5) to enable them to apply those principles in a wise way.
- They can also pray for patience as they go through the process (Col. 1:10–11).

- They can simply ask God to send them to Africa (Matt. 9:38)! In other words, they can ask God to so organize providence that they have the opportunity to serve him there.
- Specifically, they can pray that their paths will take them to a missionary society which will accept them and facilitate their service there.

'But,' Tom says, 'if providence does bring these things together as you wish, the teaching we have considered earlier must be remembered. Your acceptance by a missionary society and the providential circumstances that went with it do not constitute a message from God. He is not 'telling you' to go to Africa. You should not say that you have been specifically commissioned by God. The circumstances of providence do not contain subliminal messages. But you can rejoice that he has opened a door of service for you.'

Ben and Alice do indeed find that God opens a door of service enabling them to go to Africa. They are accepted by a missionary society, and an opportunity to serve that matches their skills arises. They want to go, they have the church's blessing, and soon they are ready.

They feel that, before they leave the UK, another meeting with Tom would be useful, to try to consolidate some of the things they have learned.

6. A godly life, a godly language

The mouth of the righteous brings forth wisdom. (Prov. 10:31)

Tom greets Ben and Alice warmly and says that he thanks God that their prayers regarding their service in Africa have been answered. Alice remarks that she is still confused sometimes by some of the things Tom has said. Most Christians she has spoken to recently truly believe that the way things have worked out mean that God really has shown them that it is his will for them to go to Africa. They believe that God has revealed his plan for their life.

But Tom challenges them to consider their situation. He reminds them that none of us knows even what tomorrow holds. He points out that they are not yet in Africa.

'God willing,' he says, 'you will go and use your gifts for him there; but imagine that you fall ill on your arrival, and after consulting medical experts, it is decided that it is not safe for you to continue in that country. Does that mean that God was mistaken? Or that God has perhaps changed his mind? The providence of your acceptance, even the answered prayers, do not mean that God is confirming his will for your future.'

Ben says that he is now not sure what he can say, and Alice asks whether it really matters anyway. Tom replies that language does matter; all language freights meaning. If you were a diabetic and your doctor was confused between hypoglycaemia and hyperglycaemia, you would become very ill—and possibly die.

Ben can see Tom's point. He thinks that, in light of what they have learned, they should avoid any statement that implies they have had a revelation from God. Such a statement, he says, suggests that we know what the future holds for us. Tom agrees, and says that this is the very thing James was saying in his letter:

> Now listen, you who say, 'Today or tomorrow we will go to this or that city, spend a year there, carry on business and make money.' Why, you do not even know what will happen tomorrow. What is your life? You are a mist that appears for a little while and then vanishes. Instead, you ought to say, 'If it is the Lord's will, we will live and do this or that.' As it is, you boast and brag. All such boasting is evil. (James 4:13–16)

James was saying that we should be careful how we speak. We should not imply that we know something we do not. Unfortunately, evangelicalism has developed its own language which is often at odds with the principles James outlines. We use phrases that convey the idea (perhaps unwittingly) of ongoing personal revelation, and so imply that God has told us something about a plan for our lives that cannot be deduced from Scripture. We frequently hear these sorts of expressions:

- I feel the Lord is telling me …
- The Lord has called me to this work.
- The Lord laid it upon my heart.
- It was the leading of the Spirit.
- I felt an inner peace that this was the right thing to do.
- I took it to the Lord in prayer (nothing wrong with that!) and (by implication) he has told me what to do.

Tom says that, in many ways, these phrases seem innocuous; certainly in his thirty-five years of Christian experience he has never known any Christian who meant to deceive when using this sort of language. But all these expressions suggest in one way or another a personal revelation, usually about some decision affecting the future direction of a believer's life.

Alice wonders what they can say about their trip to Africa. Tom replies, 'Say what you know to be true. Say that God has opened a door of service for you in Africa. And when you get there, you can then say that God has enabled you to serve him there. What is wrong with this sort of straightforward speech?'

Ben asks why people use those expressions if they are unbiblical. Part of the problem, Tom explains, is that there is confusion in the church as to what constitutes holiness. The world has always been hazy about this. To some, it is a man or woman who has taken 'holy orders' of some sort, or is simply 'religious'—although recent terrorist atrocities by 'holy' men have shaken this concept somewhat. To others, a spiritual person is one who is in mystical contact with a god or life force. But many evangelicals are similarly muddled; we talk of 'walking close to the Lord'. Our hymnology has reinforced such a concept:

When we walk with the Lord ...
Then in fellowship sweet we will sit at his feet.
Or we'll walk by his side in the way.
What he says we will do, where he sends we will go;
Never fear, only trust and obey.
(John H. Sammis)

To be in close communion in some mystical way with God, or to be receiving messages about specific life decisions, is often our measure of holiness. It all sounds spiritual, but is it? Tom asks Ben what he thinks should be the ultimate goal of the Christian. Ben offers this answer: to be Christlike.

'That's good,' says Tom; but, he continues, does that mean being like him in his earthly life? We cannot heal people on demand, speak the very words of God, calm the sea or walk on water. Nor does God expect us to. When we say 'to be Christlike', we surely mean that a Christian is to conform his or her own life to the teachings of Christ. And where are they found? The godly man is described throughout the longest psalm in the Bible as knowing, understanding and then obeying the written Word of God:

Oh, how I love your law!
  I meditate on it all day long.
Your commands make me wiser than my enemies,
  for they are ever with me.

I have more insight than all my teachers,
   for I meditate on your statutes.
I have more understanding than the elders,
   for I obey your precepts.
I have kept my feet from every evil path
   so that I might obey your word.
(Ps. 119:97–101)

And in the New Testament, Paul contrasted evil men with those who had learned the 'holy Scriptures':

> In fact, everyone who wants to live a godly life in Christ Jesus will be persecuted, while evil men and impostors will go from bad to worse, deceiving and being deceived. But as for you, continue in what you have learned and have become convinced of, because you know those from whom you learned it, and how from infancy you have known the holy Scriptures, which are able to make you wise for salvation through faith in Christ Jesus. All Scripture is God-breathed and is useful for teaching, rebuking, correcting and training in righteousness, so that the man of God may be thoroughly equipped for every good work. (2 Tim. 3:12–17)

To be Christlike, we need to know the Bible and conform our lives to it. A godly man or woman is one who knows the truth (as recorded in the Bible) and puts it into practice in his or her life.

Such a man or woman should be happy, as were the apostles, to use phrases such as 'perhaps', 'I consider', 'It seems to me' and so on, rather than the speech patterns of modern evangelicalism. Let's look at some examples:

- The circumcision issue: 'It is my judgment, therefore, that we should not make it difficult for the Gentiles who are turning to God' (James in Acts 15:19).
- The collection raised by the Corinthians: 'If it seems advisable for me to go also, they will accompany me' (Paul in 1 Cor. 16:4).
- Making plans for a missionary journey: 'Perhaps I will stay with you

awhile, or even spend the winter, so that you can help me on my journey, wherever I go' (Paul in 1 Cor. 16:6).

- Wanting Apollos to visit the Corinthian church: 'Now about our brother Apollos: I strongly urged him to go to you with the brothers. He was quite unwilling to go now, but he will go when he has the opportunity' (Paul in 1 Cor. 16:12).
- Determining how much to give: 'Each man should give what he has decided in his heart to give …' (Paul in 2 Cor. 9:7).
- Deciding to send Epaphroditus home: 'But I think it is necessary to send back to you Epaphroditus' (Paul in Phil. 2:25).
- The agony of being separated from the Thessalonians: 'So when we could stand it no longer, we thought it best to be left by ourselves in Athens. We sent Timothy …' (Paul in 1 Thes. 3:1).
- Writing to believers: 'I have much to write to you, but I do not want to use paper and ink. Instead, I hope to visit you and talk with you face to face, so that our joy may be complete' (John in 2 John 12).

Ben says, 'I suppose that this language for many sounds too rational—not spiritual—but nonetheless I can now see that it was how the apostles spoke.'

Tom tells them to consider how the first three of the Ten Commandments concern (if we can put it this way) how God feels about himself:

You shall have no other gods before me.

You shall not make for yourself an idol in the form of anything in heaven above or on the earth beneath or in the waters below. You shall not bow down to them or worship them; for I, the LORD your God, am a jealous God, punishing the children for the sin of the fathers to the third and fourth generation of those who hate me, but showing love to a thousand generations of those who love me and keep my commandments.

You shall not misuse the name of the LORD your God, for the LORD will not hold anyone guiltless who misuses his name. (Exod. 20:3–7)

Old Testament Israel had a reverence for God and his name, rooted in their understanding of Scripture. As Christians, we are in danger of losing this perspective. Many today are happy linking God's name with their own decisions, claiming that in some way he has spoken to them. But if God has not done so, surely this is a case of taking his name in vain? Even if a Christian were certain that God had so spoken to him or her, would it not be better to be more circumspect in the language used to speak of it?

The evangelical church has largely embraced a theology of a 'third way', a way somewhere between God's prescribed and decreed wills that is to be mystically determined. The implication is that Christians who are receiving messages from God to help them discover this third way are holy people, people who walk closely with Christ. Our speech patterns flow from what we believe—but they are speech patterns not found in the Bible.

Ben and Alice thank Tom and comment that they are sure to miss these times together when they are in Africa.

God's will revealed to the apostles

7. The prophetic sign gifts

Men of Israel, listen to this: Jesus of Nazareth was a man accredited by God to you by miracles, wonders and signs, which God did among you through him, as you yourselves know. (Acts 2:22)

The following year, Ben and Alice return from Africa on leave. They find that a new church has started in their neighbourhood, one that people have labelled 'charismatic'. They know of the charismatic movement but have had little experience of it first-hand, so they decide to go to one of the special meetings the church holds.

At this meeting, various people speak in strange languages; others say that they have had a word from God. At the end of the sermon, the preacher says that he knows that somebody in the congregation has a particular illness, and that this person should come and see him for healing.

What Ben and Alice are witnessing is a modern manifestation of what the Bible refers to as the gifts of tongues, prophecy, knowledge and healing. The church they have gone to teaches that all these gifts are available to any Christian 'baptized in the Holy Spirit'. It is explained to them that speaking in tongues is the gift of being able to speak in a language not previously known to the speaker, although there is usually someone present in the congregation who can interpret. Sometimes, they are told, the gift of tongues is also used as a private worship language. Prophecy is speaking the mind of God into any particular situation, and knowledge in this context is knowing something that could only have been revealed by God. Ben and Alice are told that the preacher has the gift of healing; in other words, he can say authoritatively to somebody, 'Be healed', just as Christ and the apostles did in the New Testament. This is in contrast to the ordinary Christian, who can simply pray to God and ask for somebody to be healed.

Ben is impressed: these people are so sincere, and seem so sensible. They are using language that comes straight from the Bible. And what is more, they appear to be getting a clear word from God about specific situations today. Ben wonders whether his approach is right after all. Can God's will be revealed for our life's decisions through these charismatic gifts? Alice is less sure, and they go home with much to talk about. Certainly, after his slow and sometimes painful learning curve as he came to grips with guidance teaching, Ben has resolved not to accept things second-hand, no matter how plausible they seem. So he does not need much encouragement from Alice to realize that they should do some homework. They have no hesitation in seeking help from their friend Tom, who says that they should start by clarifying some terms.

The miraculous spiritual gifts

Tom explains that the church they have visited believes that the miraculous gifts of the Spirit are present in the worldwide church today. What they have seen, he says, is a modern manifestation of the gifts of prophecy, tongues, knowledge and healing. Although today they are commonly referred to as the charismatic gifts, the word *charisma* in the New Testament meant any freely given gift. These gifts, Tom believes, were 'sign gifts' authenticating a prophet as a true spokesman of God. For that reason, he thinks they would be better described as 'prophetic gifts'. He suggests that they consider each of them in turn.

PROPHECY

The church has correctly explained to Ben and Alice that prophecy is speaking the mind of God, whether that involves predicting something or not. A prophet in the Old Testament spoke the very words of God, as can be seen from this verse in Deuteronomy: 'But a prophet who presumes to speak in my name anything I have not commanded him to say, or a prophet who speaks in the name of other gods, must be put to death' (Deut. 18:20).

Prophecy is not preaching or teaching. It is speaking the mind of God in words miraculously revealed: 'Above all, you must understand that no prophecy of Scripture came about by the prophet's own interpretation. For prophecy never had its origin in the will of man, but men spoke from God as they were carried along by the Holy Spirit' (2 Peter 1:20–21).

TONGUES

Tongues are a form of prophecy, in that the words were given to the believer by God: 'For anyone who speaks in a tongue does not speak to men but to God. Indeed, no one understands him; he utters mysteries with his spirit' (1 Cor. 14:2).

And when interpreted, a tongue had equal authority to prophecy: 'I would like every one of you to speak in tongues, but I would rather have you prophesy. He who prophesies is greater than one who speaks in tongues, unless he interprets, so that the church may be edified' (1 Cor. 14:5).

Tom further explains that, although the tongues at Pentecost were indeed recognized languages, many believers today see tongues as private worship languages, and often such believers think that these tongues are not necessarily known languages. In his first letter to the Corinthians, Paul explained that the interpretation of a tongue into a further language for the benefit of everybody listening was a separate gift (1 Cor. 12:10).

KNOWLEDGE

Tom says that the gift of knowledge was the revelation by God of a truth that could not otherwise have been known. The apostle Peter exercised this gift with Ananias and Sapphira:

Now a man named Ananias, together with his wife Sapphira, also sold a piece of property. With his wife's full knowledge he kept back part of the money for himself, but brought the rest and put it at the apostles' feet.

Then Peter said, 'Ananias, how is it that Satan has so filled your heart that you have lied to the Holy Spirit and have kept for yourself some of the money you received for the land? Didn't it belong to you before it was sold? And after it was sold, wasn't the money at your disposal? What made you think of doing such a thing? You have not lied to men but to God.'

When Ananias heard this, he fell down and died. And great fear seized all who heard what had happened. (Acts 5:1–5)

HEALING

Tom continues by telling them that the gift of healing is probably better described as the gift of healing on demand. That is the power to say authoritatively to somebody, 'Be healed', an example being found in Acts 3, when Peter healed the cripple at the temple gate.

OTHER MIRACULOUS SPIRITUAL GIFTS

Ben asks whether there were any other miraculous gifts. Tom replies that, although Christians differ on this, he considers 1 Corinthians 12 to contain a comprehensive list:

Now to each one the manifestation of the Spirit is given for the common good. To one there is given through the Spirit the message of wisdom, to another the message of knowledge by means of the same Spirit, to another faith by the same Spirit, to another gifts of healing by that one Spirit, to another miraculous powers, to another prophecy, to another distinguishing between spirits, to another speaking in different kinds of tongues, and to still another the interpretation of tongues. All these are the work of one and the same Spirit, and he gives them to each one, just as he determines. (1 Cor. 12:7–11)

Although some of these gifts have a counterpart that would not normally be termed a miraculous gift, for example, wisdom, Tom says that these all appear to him to be miraculous gifts because Paul introduced them as a 'manifestation of the Spirit'. Let's look at what Paul listed here apart from those we have already mentioned:

A MESSAGE OF WISDOM

Paul used the term 'message of wisdom', which implies a specific revelation from the Holy Spirit. This is wisdom granted to a believer beyond all powers of natural deduction.

FAITH

This does not appear to be saving faith, but a supernatural ability to believe something, which is granted to a Christian at a specific moment in time. Stephen and Barnabas are both described in Acts as being 'full of faith', so it is obviously possible to have degrees of faith.

MIRACULOUS POWERS

Paul did not specify, but this category would presumably include any remarkable power; an example would be Peter raising Tabitha from the dead (Acts 9) or Paul striking Elymas blind (Acts 13).

DISTINGUISHING BETWEEN SPIRITS

This is the God-given ability to distinguish between evil spirits and the work of the Holy Spirit. A related gift is the power to exercise authority over such evil spirits. In the Gospels, Jesus is recorded giving this power to the disciples: 'He called his twelve disciples to him and gave them authority to drive out evil spirits and to heal every disease and sickness' (Matt. 10:1).

The apostles demonstrated this gift several times in Acts, for example:

But Elymas the sorcerer (for that is what his name means) opposed them and tried to turn the proconsul from the faith. Then Saul, who was also called Paul, filled with the Holy Spirit, looked straight at Elymas and said, 'You are a child of the devil and an enemy of everything that is right! You are full of all kinds of deceit and trickery. Will you never stop perverting the right ways of the Lord? Now the hand of the Lord is against you. You are going to be blind, and for a time you will be unable to see the light of the sun.'

Immediately mist and darkness came over him, and he groped about, seeking someone to lead him by the hand. When the proconsul saw what had happened, he believed, for he was amazed at the teaching about the Lord. (Acts 13:8–12)

Miraculous spiritual gifts as signs

Tom explains that, although he believes that all these gifts had a purpose in and of themselves, they were actually all sign gifts; that is, they authenticated those who had them as being prophets of God. We see this in Jesus' conversation with Nicodemus: 'Now there was a man of the Pharisees named Nicodemus, a member of the Jewish ruling council. He came to Jesus at night and said, "Rabbi, we know you are a teacher who has come from God. For no one could perform the miraculous signs you are doing if God were not with him"' (John 3:1–2). And with the Samaritan woman:

> The woman said to him [Jesus], 'Sir, give me this water so that I won't get thirsty and have to keep coming here to draw water.'
> He told her, 'Go, call your husband and come back.'
> 'I have no husband,' she replied.
> Jesus said to her, 'You are right when you say you have no husband. The fact is, you have had five husbands, and the man you now have is not your husband. What you have just said is quite true.'
> 'Sir,' the woman said, 'I can see that you are a prophet.' (John 4:15–19)

So both Nicodemus (referred to by Christ as 'Israel's teacher') and the lowly Samaritan woman saw that a prophet was authenticated by miraculous signs.

In Acts we specifically read: 'Men of Israel, listen to this: Jesus of Nazareth was a man accredited by God to you by miracles, wonders and signs, which God did among you through him, as you yourselves know' (Acts 2:22).

Non-apostolic gifting

Ben points out that many people in the New Testament seemed to be able to do miraculous things; in the passage they have considered from

1 Corinthians, Paul said that the gifts were given to each one for the common good. This is what Ben and Alice's new friends have said: that these gifts are for ordinary church members. And, Ben continues, with these gifts it is possible to find God's will today directly, not just from Scripture. In reply, Tom says that the Corinthian Christians did indeed possess these miraculous gifts. But throughout biblical history, these gifts and abilities served as authenticating signs that the people who possessed them were prophets—from Moses, through the time of Elijah, down to Christ, the apostles, and the New Testament prophets we read about in Corinth.

Alice asks how they might make sense of all this. Tom says that a key to understanding this issue is to understand the role, gifts and office of an apostle.

'I suggest,' he says, 'that we start at the beginning of Acts and look at the events surrounding Pentecost—the "birthday" of the church.'

Let us see how they fare.

8. The unique apostolic gifting

But when he, the Spirit of truth, comes, he will guide you into all truth. He will not speak on his own; he will speak only what he hears, and he will tell you what is yet to come. (John 16:13)

Pentecost was for the apostles only

Tom explains that there are two lessons he wants Ben and Alice to learn. The first is that at Pentecost, it was only the apostles who experienced the tongues of fire and were filled with the Holy Spirit:

> Then they cast lots, and the lot fell to Matthias; so he was added to the eleven apostles.
>
> When the day of Pentecost came, they were all together in one place. Suddenly a sound like the blowing of a violent wind came from heaven and filled the whole house where they were sitting. They saw what seemed to be tongues of fire that separated and came to rest on each of them. All of them were filled with the Holy Spirit and began to speak in other tongues as the Spirit enabled them. (Acts 1:26—2:4)

The context makes it clear that the pronouns 'they' and 'them' in 2:1–4 must refer to the subject (the 'eleven') of 1:26. The rather awkward chapter split, which was not in the original text, somewhat obscures this point. That this is the case is further emphasized by them all being described as Galileans—as the apostles were (Acts 1:11; 2:7).

We should not be surprised by this, explains Tom, because Jesus repeatedly promised that something special was going to happen to them:

> I have much more to say to you, more than you can now bear. But when he, the Spirit of truth, comes, he will guide you into all truth. He will not speak on his own; he will speak only what he hears, and he will tell you what is yet to come. He will bring glory to me by taking from what is mine and making it known to you. All that belongs to the Father is mine. That is why I said the Spirit will take from what is mine and make it known to you. (John 16:12–15)

Jesus repeated this promise again just before his bodily ascension into heaven:

> 'Do not leave Jerusalem, but wait for the gift my Father promised, which you have heard me speak about. For John baptised with water, but in a few days you will be baptised with the Holy Spirit.'

> So when they met together, they asked him, 'Lord, are you at this time going to restore the kingdom to Israel?'

> He said to them: 'It is not for you to know the times or dates the Father has set by his own authority. But you will receive power when the Holy Spirit comes on you; and you will be my witnesses in Jerusalem, and in all Judea and Samaria, and to the ends of the earth.' (Acts 1:4–8)

At Pentecost, the disciples spoke in languages known to the people present but that they themselves had not previously learned (2:7–8). The lowly and often-confused disciples now became the wonder-working apostles! They were later described in the New Testament as the foundation of the church of God:

> Consequently, you are no longer foreigners and aliens, but fellow-

citizens with God's people and members of God's household, built on the foundation of the apostles and prophets, with Christ Jesus himself as the chief cornerstone. In him the whole building is joined together and rises to become a holy temple in the Lord. And in him you too are being built together to become a dwelling in which God lives by his Spirit. (Eph. 2:19–22)

The Pentecostal experience was just for them—not for all those present at Pentecost.

But Ben points out that Peter, in his sermon, said that the Pentecostal experience was for all: 'Peter replied, "Repent and be baptised, every one of you, in the name of Jesus Christ for the forgiveness of your sins. And you will receive the gift of the Holy Spirit. The promise is for you and your children and for all who are far off—for all whom the Lord our God will call"' (Acts 2:38–39).

'Yes,' says Tom, 'the "gift of the Holy Spirit" is for us all—but not necessarily everything else the apostles experienced. Great care needs to be taken when the book of Acts is being studied, as it records a transitional period in church history. The events described follow on directly from the Gospels, in that at the beginning of Acts, Jesus is still on earth, albeit in his resurrection body. Just as we do not expect Jesus to rise from the dead each Easter Sunday, and we do not expect to see him walking around today in his resurrection body, so we must not expect all the events of Acts to be replicated in our day.'

'So what is this "gift of the Spirit"?' asks Ben.

'It is the "baptism in the Spirit",' replies Tom. 'The terms are interchangeable in these verses.'

Baptism in the Spirit is for all Christians

Tom's first point was that Pentecost was for the apostles only; his second point is that, in contrast, the baptism in the Spirit (the gift of the Spirit) is for all believers. John the Baptist's promise was clear—it was repeated in all four Gospels: 'I baptise you with water for repentance. But after me will come one [Christ] who is more powerful than I, whose sandals I am not fit to carry. He will baptise you with the Holy Spirit and with fire' (Matt. 3:11).

Ben says, 'Look, we are told to expect those tongues of fire—just like the apostles!' Tom suggests that, again, this specific promise was fulfilled only with the apostles at Pentecost. He knows of no Christian group that claims that we should all experience tongues of fire. But when Paul wrote to the Christian believers at Corinth, he made the very point that Tom is trying to make: that every believer is baptized in the Spirit. 'For we were all baptised by one Spirit into one body—whether Jews or Greeks, slave or free—and we were all given the one Spirit to drink' (1 Cor. 12:13).

Tom says that, if we now look carefully at all these verses, we can deduce:

- It is Christ who baptizes in (or by or with) the Holy Spirit.
- Every Christian has this baptism, as Paul made clear in 1 Corinthians 12:13.
- But not every Christian so baptized will speak in tongues. In the same chapter, Paul asked rhetorically, 'Are all apostles? Are all prophets? Are all teachers? Do all work miracles? Do all have gifts of healing? Do all speak in tongues? Do all interpret? But eagerly desire the greater gifts' (vv. 29–31). He obviously expected the answer 'no'!
- So all Christians in the church era would be baptized with the Spirit—they would all receive the 'promise', as Peter called it in his first great sermon after Pentecost—but not every Christian would experience exactly what the apostles experienced. For example, they would not all speak in tongues.

So, Tom says, we can now see that at Pentecost:

- The apostles were baptized by Christ in the Spirit promised by Christ. It was their initiation into full Christian life. These apostles were the first Christians of the church age—it was the 'birthday' of the church.
- But at the same time, the apostles had received their unique apostolic gifting, as Jesus had promised in John 16 and elsewhere. This is evidenced by the fact that immediately afterwards they did indeed become infallible, authoritative communicators of God's truth.

Alice and Ben can see that this is clear New Testament teaching, not a series of deductions made from different experiences that happened to the apostles and others in a transitional period of history. They believe that what they have learned is a benchmark by which the various accounts of the reception of the charismatic gifts in Acts should be judged.

The gift of tongues

Ben then asks for more clarification about the tongues gift. Tom explains that Jews from many nations, speaking many different languages, had gathered for the feast of Pentecost, and each now heard at least one apostle 'speaking in his own language' (Acts 2:6). It was prophesied in Isaiah 28 that the Jews would indeed one day hear the Word of God in a language that was not their own: 'Very well then, with foreign lips and strange tongues God will speak to this people …' (v. 11). Then, some years later, when Paul was writing to the Corinthians about spiritual gifts, he gave this explanation, quoting Isaiah 28:

> In the Law it is written:
> 'Through men of strange tongues
>   and through the lips of foreigners
> I will speak to this people,
>   but even then they will not listen to me,'
> says the Lord.

Tongues, then, are a sign, not for believers but for unbelievers; prophecy, however, is for believers, not for unbelievers' (1 Cor. 14:21–22).

A sign for unbelieving Jews

Alice asks who these unbelievers were. Tom says that, because of Paul's reference to Isaiah 28, it appears that they were unbelieving Jews. He refers Alice to Paul's letter to the Romans, where Paul explained that the Jew who trusted in his physical descent from Abraham was a Jew by race only:

It is not as though God's word had failed. For not all who are descended from Israel are Israel. Nor because they are his descendants are they all Abraham's children. On the contrary, 'It is through Isaac that your offspring will be reckoned.' In other words, it is not the natural children who are God's children, but it is the children of the promise who are regarded as Abraham's offspring. (Rom. 9:6–8)

In other words, 'a man is a Jew if he is one inwardly; and circumcision is circumcision of the heart, by the Spirit, not by the written code' (Rom. 2:29).

So, Tom explains, a true Jew is one who trusts in God. Such Jewish believers would, of course, recognize that belonging to God was a matter of faith, not a matter of genealogy, and would presumably have no problem with Gentiles coming to faith in God. Paul, with his application of Isaiah 28, seemed to be saying that the tongues at Pentecost (and, some believe, every manifestation of tongues in the New Testament) were a sign to unbelieving Jews that the gospel was for the Gentiles as well as the Jews.

The tongues were a sign that Pentecost really was a turning point in history: despite in the past dealing principally with the Jewish nation, God's heart had always been towards the Gentiles, and now the gospel was going to be carried out to all the world with God's blessing and in the Holy Spirit's power. [1]

'So,' asks Ben, 'is this the reason why you are not convinced that the gift of tongues is for today?'

'It's one among several reasons,' replies Tom. But he continues: 'Whatever you believe about tongues, you must remember that, as we have seen, they had a prophetic element in them; the speaker was speaking words supplied by God.' Tom then explains that the whole 'tongues' thing is a big subject, but one Ben and Alice can easily research, as many books have been written about it. Instead, Ben and Alice decide to move on in their study. They will only come back to consider tongues if they agree that it is a gift for today.

Alice says that she now realizes more clearly than before that the apostles occupied a unique place in the history of the church, but she cannot see the significance of this in relation to the charismatic gifts today. Has she missed something?

Tom suggests that, starting with Acts 8, they look more closely at what made an apostle an apostle. He advises them to look carefully at the incidents recorded there in light of the clear teaching elsewhere in the New Testament.

Notes

1. This argument is further strengthened by 1 Corinthians 14:2: 'For anyone who speaks in a tongue does not speak to men but to God. Indeed, no one understands him; he utters mysteries with his spirit.' The word 'mystery' in the New Testament refers to the inclusion of the Gentiles in the promises of God. See especially **Victor Budgen,** *The Charismatics and the Word of God* (Darlington: Evangelical Press, 1989), p. 47ff.

9. The unique apostolic gift

The things that mark an apostle—signs, wonders and miracles—were done among you with great perseverance. (2 Cor. 12:12)

Acts 8

Ben and Alice go away, wondering what they are to see in this chapter. They soon read:

Simon himself believed and was baptised. And he followed Philip everywhere, astonished by the great signs and miracles he saw.

When the apostles in Jerusalem heard that Samaria had accepted the word of God, they sent Peter and John to them. When they arrived, they prayed for them that they might receive the Holy Spirit, because the Holy Spirit had not yet come upon any of them; they had simply been baptised into the name of the Lord Jesus. Then Peter and John placed their hands on them, and they received the Holy Spirit.

When Simon saw that the Spirit was given at the laying on of the apostles' hands, he offered them money and said, 'Give me also this ability so that everyone on whom I lay my hands may receive the Holy Spirit.' (Acts 8:13–19)

Ben says that these are the very things the charismatic church has told them about—that when Christians have hands laid on them, they are baptized in the Spirit and receive the miraculous gifts. Alice reminds Ben that they have promised Tom not to jump to conclusions, but instead to look carefully at these incidents in the light of other clear New Testament teaching. They decide to sequence the events recorded in Acts 8:

- Philip is a wonder-working Christian, but not an apostle.
- He preaches the gospel in Samaria.
- Some are converted—Philip considers them to be believers.
- As believers, they must already possess the Spirit.
- The apostles come from Jerusalem and lay their hands on these believers; they then 'receive the Spirit'.
- Simon asks for that gift.

Alice points out that the converted Christians must already have been 'baptized in the Spirit' if they were Christians at all—Paul is so clear about that in 1 Corinthians 12:13. So why were these believers baptized in the Spirit again? Perhaps they were not yet Christians after all? But Ben thinks that the whole tenor of Acts 8 suggests that they were indeed already genuine believers; certainly Philip thought they were. Alice agrees.

Then Alice sees it: the passage doesn't say that, when the apostles laid hands on these believers, they were 'baptized in the Spirit'; merely that they 'received the Holy Spirit'. Furthermore, she says, this must have been something visible; Simon saw what the apostles had done and wanted it! Baptism in the Spirit is not a visible thing: it is when a believer is brought to faith in Christ and incorporated into the worldwide eternal church. Baptism in the Spirit is a spiritual reality, not a visible, earthly one; 'receiving the Spirit' must, therefore, be referring to something else, something visible or audible—but what can it be? Alice suggests to Ben that it must be the tongues gift. At the first Pentecost, everybody marvelled at that gift; it was there for those present to see and hear.

Ben thinks that Alice is on to something; receiving the Spirit is not about baptism in the Spirit at all—it is about receiving spiritual gifts. Eventually, Alice asks why Simon didn't ask Philip for the Spirit. Doesn't the passage say that Simon was amazed at the signs and miracles Philip did?

Then Ben realizes that the answer is in the passage itself: it was through the laying on of the apostles' hands that the Spirit was given. Philip could not do it; he could not give the spiritual gifts to another—he was not an apostle, but one man among others commissioned by the apostles: 'This proposal pleased the whole group. They chose Stephen, a man full of faith and of the Holy Spirit; also Philip, Procorus, Nicanor, Timon, Parmenas, and Nicolas from Antioch, a convert to Judaism. They presented these men to the apostles, who prayed and laid their hands on them' (Acts 6:5–6).

When Ben shares this thought with Alice, she astutely points out that Simon did not actually ask for the gifts; what he had said was: 'Give me also this ability so that everyone on whom I lay my hands may receive the Holy Spirit.'

Suddenly Ben has it. What Simon was asking for was the apostolic ability to transmit the gifts. He explains to Alice that the term 'simony' means the selling of a church office. He says that it was common practice in the Middle Ages to sell, say, a bishopric, so that the incumbent could benefit from its associated income. The fact that this practice was called simony must mean that this is the historic understanding of what was happening in Acts 8: Simon was, in effect, offering to pay to be an apostle; he was asking for the apostolic office and the transmission gift associated with it.

Alice says, 'I think you must be right. Something was happening here that only the apostles could do. Whatever it was, it could not be about giving these disciples saving faith; if only the original apostles could give saving faith, and that by physical contact, there would be very few Christians indeed! Peter and John did something that had an immediate, visible effect, just as at the apostolic Pentecost. It was something Philip could not do.'

Ben and Alice decide to recapitulate what have they learned so far:
- Jesus promised the disciples that they would receive a special baptism and be led into 'all truth'.
- This happened at Pentecost, when they were each baptized in the Spirit. The disciples were transitional believers—born in the Old Testament era, now fully fledged Christians.
- At this Pentecost, the disciples also received new spiritual gifts that

included the gift of tongues. Paul explained that it was a sign gift that
the gospel was for all—Jew and Gentile alike.

- Furthermore, the disciples received their apostolic gifting. This
included the ability to teach Christian truth infallibly.
- The disciples also received the unique ability to transmit spiritual
gifts to others.
- In Peter's first great sermon after his own apostolic gifting, he
promised that all believers would now receive the *gift* of the Holy
Spirit, not the *gifts* of the Holy Spirit (Acts 2:38).
- This is in harmony with what Paul taught in 1 Corinthians 12: that
all believers in the church age are baptized in the Spirit, although
not all would necessarily have spiritual gifts.
- Some believers (such as Philip) could do wonders using the new
spiritual gifts, but they could not transmit the gifts to others.

But is Ben and Alice's understanding of these things correct? They
decide to make a trip back to see Tom. He agrees with their analysis and
points out that, even if the traditional 'charismatic' interpretation of Acts 8
were correct—that the believers in Samaria were baptized in the Spirit
when they had hands laid on them—the death knell to this teaching is
heard in the same passage: it was clearly only the original apostles who
could perform this act, a fact which is rarely mentioned in any
charismatic literature.

Tom suggests that Ben and Alice go and do some more study together
and see if what they have deduced is corroborated not only by the events
of Acts themselves, but also by the clear teaching given elsewhere in the
New Testament. They soon come across Acts 9.

The Damascus road

Ben and Alice read the story of Saul's dramatic conversion on the road to
Damascus and the task Ananias was given:

> But the Lord said to Ananias, 'Go! This man is my chosen instrument
> to carry my name before the Gentiles and their kings and before the
> people of Israel. I will show him how much he must suffer for my
> name.'

Then Ananias went to the house and entered it. Placing his hands on Saul, he said, 'Brother Saul, the Lord—Jesus, who appeared to you on the road as you were coming here—has sent me so that you may see again and be filled with the Holy Spirit.' Immediately, something like scales fell from Saul's eyes, and he could see again. He got up and was baptised ... (Acts 9:15–18)

Alice says that this, in her opinion, confirms her view that Saul (soon to be called Paul) was the missing apostle. He—and not Matthias—was Christ's choice to make up the twelve. We can see that Paul was met personally by Christ and left blind by the encounter. Ananias was subsequently told by Christ specifically to visit Paul and lay hands on him to heal him of his blindness (v. 12). Ananias did as he was instructed and Paul was filled with the Holy Spirit. Alice says that she can see it was Christ who chose and commissioned Paul, not Ananias—he was simply the messenger. She considers this to have been Paul's personal Pentecost, and therefore does not feel that it could set a precedent. Ben thinks that this is a reasonable explanation, but is less sure about Matthias being a wrong choice.

The very next chapter brings them to the events at the house of Cornelius.

Cornelius

Cornelius had a vision; an angel told him to send men to Peter's house. When they arrived, they found Peter, who, although often seen as impetuous and headstrong, was reflecting on a lesson he had just received directly from God. In the vision, animals that were unclean according to Jewish law had been lowered down to him on a sheet and he had been told to kill and eat them. He had protested, but God had told him not to call impure what God had made clean (Acts 10:9–15).

It was just at this moment that the men Cornelius had sent arrived at his door. Peter went with them back to Cornelius's house and told the large gathering of Gentiles and Jews there, in light of the vision God had given him, 'I now realise how true it is that God does not show favouritism but accepts men from every nation who fear him and do what is right' (vv. 34–35).

Peter had got the message; it was the same message that should have been learned from the tongues in Acts 2: they were a sign that the old division between the Gentile and the Jew was finished. As Peter continued to tell his story, his audience (Jews and Gentiles), to his surprise, began speaking in tongues: 'While Peter was still speaking these words, the Holy Spirit came on all who heard the message. The circumcised believers who had come with Peter were astonished that the gift of the Holy Spirit had been poured out even on the Gentiles. For they heard them speaking in tongues and praising God' (vv. 44–46).

Peter saw that the miraculous gift of tongues had been given to others, just as it had been in Samaria—but this time, it seems, not through the laying on of an apostle's hands, but in the same way the disciples had received it at the first Pentecost. This is the only recorded exception in the New Testament to the principle of the apostolic transmission of the miraculous spiritual gifts. It is an understandable one, Peter would not of his own volition have laid his hands on the Gentiles for them to receive the gifts—it was the very lesson he was being taught: the Gentiles were included in the promised outpouring of the Holy Spirit. He declared: 'Can anyone keep these people from being baptised with water? They have received the Holy Spirit just as we have' (v. 47). He obviously considered the receipt of the miraculous gift of tongues to mean that they had received the gift of the Holy Spirit, so he suggested that they be baptized.

So this remarkable event was like another Pentecost, only in Cornelius' sitting room! But Ben and Alice can see that there were several differences:

- In the house of Cornelius, the recipients simultaneously came to faith in Christ (at the first Pentecost, the apostles were already believers in Christ).
- The recipients did not receive apostolic gifting.
- The recipients were not led into 'all truth'.
- This was not the 'birthday' of the church.

The nature of the events recorded in Acts 10 indicates that they had one purpose: to teach Peter, and through him the other apostles, that the division between Jew and Gentile had come to an end. News of the event spread to the other apostles and throughout Judea. In Acts 11, Peter carefully related the whole incident to the Jewish believers in Jerusalem.

It was a key moment in the early history of the church. Ben and Alice agree that the apostolic Pentecost, Christ's dramatic appearance to Paul on the road to Damascus and the events at the house of Cornelius do not set a pattern for the church age.

They continue their reading in Acts but find no further instances of anybody receiving the miraculous spiritual gifts until Acts 19, which, they discover, records events that took place more than twenty years after the apostolic Pentecost.

Acts 19

While Apollos was at Corinth, Paul took the road through the interior and arrived at Ephesus. There he found some disciples and asked them, 'Did you receive the Holy Spirit when you believed?'

They answered, 'No, we have not even heard that there is a Holy Spirit.'

So Paul asked, 'Then what baptism did you receive?'

'John's baptism,' they replied.

Paul said, 'John's baptism was a baptism of repentance. He told the people to believe in the one coming after him, that is, in Jesus.'

On hearing this, they were baptised into the name of the Lord Jesus. When Paul placed his hands on them, the Holy Spirit came on them, and they spoke in tongues and prophesied. (Acts 19:1–6)

Ben and Alice can see that the situation here was different from that in Samaria as recorded in Acts 8. These Ephesian disciples were not believers; they were disciples of John the Baptist. Paul taught them the gospel, they believed (and therefore must have been baptized in the Spirit), they were baptized in water, and then Paul (an apostle) laid hands on them and they received the miraculous spiritual gifts, speaking in tongues and prophesying.

To Ben and Alice, this clearly confirms what they have learned, and presents the same sequence of events as Acts 8, where Peter and John were the apostolic representatives. The only difference is that, on this occasion, the disciples were not Christian believers when the apostle Paul arrived. Ben and Alice set out the events as follows:

Acts 8
- The gospel is preached by Philip to some people in Samaria.
- They come to faith in Christ.
- They are baptized in water.
- The apostles Peter and John arrive and lay hands on them, and the believers receive the miraculous gifts.

Acts 19
- The gospel is preached by Paul to some people in Ephesus.
- They come to faith in Christ.
- They are baptized in water.
- The apostle Paul lays hands on them, and the believers receive the miraculous gifts.

Gifts—false and true?

Ben and Alice now realize why Tom had directed them to Acts 8. If the miraculous spiritual gifts were transmitted only by the original apostles, as that passage indicates, then there can be no such gifts today. But this causes a problem for Alice: she wants to know what to make of the use of the gifts by some Christians today. One of her new friends, an especially devout Christian, speaks in tongues regularly. So when Ben and Alice next meet with Tom, this is the first question she asks.

Tom says that he knew that, sooner or later, they would ask this. The problem is that, even as evangelicals, we look at Scripture through a screen of our experience and culture.

'I suppose that will always be the case,' he says. 'Nonetheless, we should do our best when studying the Bible to see what Scripture is actually saying. So let's consider this subject now, otherwise we might not be able to see clearly the Bible's teaching in any subsequent study together.'

Tom then says to Alice, 'I know a man, a devout Christian, who gets drunk every night.'

Alice replies that that must be wrong because the Bible speaks against drunkenness.

'Actually, I'm teasing you,' says Tom. 'But do you see? You quite rightly used the Bible as your reference point to judge whether drunkenness was of God or not. We should do this whether we are considering drunkenness or speaking in tongues.'

Tom goes on to say that, from Bible times until now, people in all sorts of faith communities, Christian and non-Christian, have practised many different signs and wonders, including faith healing, prophesying and speaking in tongues. Every believer has to decide how to evaluate these, and whether it is the Bible or experience that is going to be the final judge as to which are manifestations of the Holy Spirit, and which are not.

'One problem,' says Tom, 'is that, in our postmodern world, the concept of absolute truth has often been abandoned. Your own thoughts and experiences are what make reality for you; mine will be different, so they will be my reality. In other words, the concept of an objective truth is pushed to one side. This is why so many have embraced "spirituality" and yet rejected religion. Orthodox Christianity, certainly since the Reformation, has looked to stand on the Bible alone. In other words, any experience has to be brought to the Bible to decide whether it is true or false.'

'But any experience is true for the person who has experienced it!' says Alice.

Tom agrees. But what he means is that any experience, no matter how real to the person, does not necessarily represent an objective reality. Alice says that she is now getting lost in the argument.

'Well,' says Tom, 'consider dreams. They are often incredibly vivid. In a dream, you might have killed your own mother—but (thankfully) when you wake up, you haven't. The dream did not represent what was true. It was not "real"; it was entirely a product of the subconscious mind. And although some try to attach meanings to dreams, to most of us they remain a mystery.'

'Yes, I understand now what you're saying,' says Alice. 'If I based my beliefs on the content of my dreams, I would have a very strange belief system indeed!'

'That's right,' says Tom, 'me, too!' He goes on to explain how we check the content of a dream by the reality we experience upon waking, and the reality wins the day—at least, for most people! And so it is—or should be—with believers and the Bible. If they experience something that they believe to be from God, they should check in the Bible to see if it is.

Tom gives an example. A woman comes to faith in Christ and she experiences an enormous sense of relief that her past sins, which were many, are forgiven. She reads in the Bible and finds that it is true: her sins really have been forgiven! We can assure her that she has experienced a genuine Christian emotion. Her emotion is a reflection of an objective reality. In contrast, an unbelieving woman goes to a spiritualist. She is also told that her sins are forgiven. She, too, then experiences an enormous sense of relief. But it is false. She has not embraced Christ as her Saviour; whatever peace she may experience, no sins have been forgiven.

The Bible is like an anvil on which every Christian experience is proven. In other words, we do not have an experience and then modify what we believe accordingly; instead, we check it against the Bible.

Alice comments that it still bothers her to think that some of her friends may, in some way, have been deceived by these miraculous gift experiences. She points out that some in their own church think that these things come from the devil. Is that what Tom thinks?

In reply, he says that, in many sincere Bible-based charismatic churches where prophesying and tongue speaking are accepted, the eldership exercises some sort of control whereby the prophecy or tongue has to be 'tested' and confirmed. In other words, the elders at such churches themselves accept that not all such experiences are from God. Tom says that there is no need to speculate on some sinister source, any more than we would with our dreams.

'Every charismatic fellowship I know of has problems with false prophecies and spurious tongues, so why not ask your friends where such things come from in their own church?' he suggests. 'I am confident that they will reassure you that the false prophecy or tongue was simply a mistake—a misunderstanding by the person involved, who was probably only wanting to be useful in the fellowship by sharing something believed to have been given by God.'

Apostolic gift transmission

Ben still expresses some doubt that the Bible as a whole teaches that the miraculous gifts were transmitted exclusively by the apostles and so are not for today. Tom gives them some further verses to look at:

> I long to see you so that I may impart to you some spiritual gift to make you strong. (Rom. 1:11)

They consider what Paul was saying here. Tom says that Paul was writing in AD 55 to the church at Rome to encourage, challenge and teach the people there. But there seems to have been something he could not do for them—impart some spiritual gift—unless he was actually present with them. It is now not difficult for Ben and Alice to see what this is referring to. Paul could not transmit any spiritual gift unless he laid hands on them. It is possible that some at Rome could already prophesy (see Rom. 12:6), but many commentators today believe that the church at Rome had never been visited by an apostle; rather, it had been founded by Jews and proselytes who had been in Jerusalem at the time of the apostolic Pentecost (Acts 2:10–11). Ben agrees that it is actually very difficult to make sense of the verse unless Paul was saying that he had to be present to transmit a miraculous spiritual gift.

> Do not neglect your gift, which was given you through a prophetic message when the body of elders laid their hands on you. (1 Tim. 4:14)

> For this reason I remind you to fan into flame the gift of God, which is in you through the laying on of my hands. (2 Tim. 1:6)

Tom says that in both verses Paul is writing to Timothy. Was he referring to two separate events or one? Alice thinks, and Ben concedes, that Paul was referring to one and the same event. The passages refer to one gift—'the gift' and 'your gift'—not two or more gifts. It seems that Paul was present with the other elders when hands were laid on the young pastor. In 1 Timothy, through modesty, Paul did not specify that actually it was he, the apostle, who had personally transmitted the gift—a point he clarified in 2 Timothy.

Do not be hasty in the laying on of hands, and do not share in the sins of others. Keep yourself pure. (1 Tim. 5:22)

Tom asks whether this meant that Timothy could now lay hands on believers and transmit the spiritual gifts. But Ben points out that the verse does not say that; no other verse in the New Testament suggests it either, and, if true, it would certainly seem to contradict what Simon deduced in Acts 8. Ben and Alice agree, and decide that, unless they come across clear teaching to suggest that others had the apostolic transmission gift, they would consider this laying on of hands to be a symbolic gesture, carried out by elders on a believer when commissioning him or her for some gospel work, just as those early church elders did with Timothy. Ben and Alice know that many churches today do a similar thing.

Tom gives Ben and Alice one more passage to consider, this time from 2 Corinthians, where Paul is making a passionate defence to the Corinthian believers of his claim to be recognized as an apostle:

I have made a fool of myself, but you drove me to it. I ought to have been commended by you, for I am not in the least inferior to the 'super-apostles', even though I am nothing. The things that mark an apostle—signs, wonders and miracles—were done among you with great perseverance. (2 Cor. 12:11–12)

Ben and Alice leave Tom's, wondering what this passage might hold for them. When they have a chance to examine it, Ben quickly sees that Paul must be referring to a unique apostolic gift. Many others could do 'signs, wonders and miracles'—Acts 8 clearly describes the miraculous ministry of Philip, not an apostle: 'When the crowds heard Philip and saw the miraculous signs he did, they all paid close attention to what he said' (8:6); 'Simon himself believed and was baptised. And he followed Philip everywhere, astonished by the great signs and miracles he saw' (8:13). And even the ordinary believers at Corinth, despite all their faults, did not lack the spiritual gifts: 'Therefore you do not lack any spiritual gift as you eagerly wait for our Lord Jesus Christ to be revealed' (1 Cor. 1:7).

Ben considers that Paul must have been referring to his ability to transmit the miraculous gifts. Acts 6:5–6 specifically says that the apostles had laid their hands on Philip—this must have been the source of his miraculous gifts—but nonetheless he could not transmit the gifts and neither, presumably, could the Corinthians or the 'super-apostles'. It could be that these 'super-apostles' were actually mimicking the transmission gift, which is perhaps why Paul gave them that name.

The ability to transmit the gifts was indeed the 'mark of an apostle'. It was a sign gift that Paul could confidently use to 'trump' any other wonder-worker and so-called apostle. Alice agrees; she thinks that it could not be anything else.

10. The unique apostolic office

Am I not free? Am I not an apostle? Have I not seen Jesus our Lord? Are you not the result of my work in the Lord? (1 Cor. 9:1)

When Ben and Alice next meet with Tom, he explains to them that it is important to understand not just apostolic gifting but also the qualifications for apostolic office. The New Testament, he says, refers to apostles in a general sense; the word 'apostle' simply means 'one who is sent', a sort of messenger, as well as apostles in a specific sense: those who were sent by Christ. So, although not commissioned by Christ, Barnabas is referred to as an apostle (Acts 14:14). Tom says that, in a way, not belonging to the original apostolic band chosen by Christ was a problem for Paul: he was sensitive to this fact, and this explains some of his comments, for example: 'Am I not free? Am I not an apostle? Have I not seen Jesus our Lord? Are you not the result of my work in the Lord?' (1 Cor. 9:1). Here Paul was saying that he had seen the (risen) Lord. This, of course, happened on the Damascus road, when Christ personally commissioned him. He further said, 'Then he [Christ] appeared to James, then to all the apostles, and last of all he appeared to me also, as to one abnormally born' (1 Cor. 15:7–8).

Alice asks what 'abnormally born' meant.

'Born at the wrong time,' Tom explains. Paul missed out on being a disciple during Christ's earthly ministry and Christ had to commission him as an apostle much later than the others. Paul's comment that Christ appeared to him last of all is a reference to his Damascus road experience.

Some believe that this means that Christ has never appeared to anyone else since, so any subsequent claim of a vision of Christ by any believer is spurious.

Ben relates Alice's theory that Paul was the intended twelfth apostle. Tom says that that makes sense. He points out that Matthias was not commissioned by Christ—he was chosen by the other apostles, and that after they cast lots. The New Testament never refers to Matthias as an apostle, only that he was 'added to the eleven apostles' (Acts 1:26). Tom says that simply being counted in their number did not make him a true apostle.

'When I was a young boy,' he says, 'I spent so much time with my school friend, staying at his home and going on holiday with him, that I was counted as a member of his family; but of course I wasn't. Indeed Barnabas, as we have seen, was counted among the apostles but nonetheless did not truly belong to the Twelve. Jesus had specifically told the disciples to wait until the Spirit guided them into "all truth" (John 16:13), but they didn't; they chose Matthias before they received their apostolic gifting.' Tom reminds Ben that the Bible often records historical events that are not according to God's prescribed will.

Ben can see the point. Apostles were considered infallible teachers of the church—its very foundation (Eph. 2:20). If it were possible for anybody other than Christ to appoint an apostle, there could be no definitive number of apostles—and therefore no definitive body of truth for Christians to believe. And yet the New Testament speaks as if there is such a defined and complete teaching: 'Dear friends, although I was very eager to write to you about the salvation we share, I felt I had to write and urge you to contend for the faith that was once for all entrusted to the saints' (Jude 3). Also, Ben knows enough about the Roman Catholic Church to realize that this is the very basis of their papacy (that one apostle could appoint another), the present pope apparently standing in a line from Peter himself. And, like Peter, the pope today is considered by Roman Catholics to be able to teach infallibly the words of Christ. So all Roman Catholics today accept that their faith is not 'once for all entrusted to the saints', but is rather developing and changing.

Tom says that Christians need to understand that, although the New

Covenant is embedded in the Old, and that the New Testament is impossible to explain without the Old, in the church age, God was making a break with the past: he was doing a 'new thing', a fact repeatedly referred to in the New Testament (e.g. Matt. 9:17; Mark 1:27; Heb. 8:13). This included the way he was going to reveal himself to men and women: 'In the past God spoke to our forefathers through the prophets at many times and in various ways, but in these last days he has spoken to us by his Son, whom he appointed heir of all things, and through whom he made the universe' (Heb. 1:1–2).

Previously, revelation, although intermittent, was an ongoing experience for Israel as God progressively explained his purposes. Over the centuries, priests, kings and prophets came and went. But all this came to a climax in Christ. Hebrews teaches that Christ is our great High Priest, and the book of Revelation describes Christ as the King of kings (Rev. 17:14; 19:16; also 1 Tim. 6:15). Furthermore, Christ is the great prophet of which Deuteronomy speaks: 'The LORD your God will raise up for you a prophet like me from among your own brothers. You must listen to him' (Deut. 18:15).

Believers generally are not expecting another high priest or another heavenly king; nor should they expect another prophet. Revelation is no longer progressive—Christ is the end point of revelation for the church age.

Now we know that Christ did not himself commit his teaching to written form, so there had to be those who followed him to undertake the task. Peter, in his second letter, repeatedly reminded his recipients of the importance of Scripture and said, 'I want you to recall the words spoken in the past by the holy prophets and the command given by our Lord and Saviour through your apostles' (2 Peter 3:2). In other words, Christ's teaching came via the apostles. They, or those they had authorized (e.g. Luke and Mark), were Christ's earthly representatives appointed to write the New Testament. Every Christian prophet or Scripture author could trace his authority directly back to Christ through the apostles, as each had received his prophetic gift from an apostle or had his writing endorsed by an apostle, each apostle being personally commissioned by Christ and given authenticating miraculous gifts by him.

In that sense, then, Christ authored the New Testament and put his imprimatur on it. Modern-day prophecy breaks this crucial link between prophecy, the authenticating miraculous gifts and the apostles, and so directly with Christ, because there can be no apostolic commissioning of prophets today.

Ben now has to admit that these New Testament verses do seem to back up their initial conclusions from their study in Acts. But it is such an important teaching that he wants to see more clear evidence. Tom asks him what else he wants to see. Ben replies that he would be convinced if he saw clear teaching from the Bible that the miraculous gifts would stop after the last apostle died, and that the New Testament made it clear that there would be no more prophetic revelation.

Tom says that that is enough for today, but gives them their homework: 1 Corinthians 13:8–13. Ben says that he knows that passage: it is all about love.

Alice suspects that that might not be the whole story.

God's will recorded in Scripture

11. A complete revelation

Love never fails. But where there are prophecies, they will cease; where there are tongues, they will be stilled; where there is knowledge, it will pass away. (1 Cor. 13:8)

1 Corinthians 13:8–13

Ben and Alice think that they know what this passage is about: when Christ returns in glory, faith and hope will cease but love will last for ever in heaven; that is why love is the 'greatest' of the three. But by now they know Tom well enough to realize that he would not have given them a passage without good reason, so they decide to look at it carefully and see what it actually says, not what they think it says:

Love never fails. But where there are prophecies, they will cease; where there are tongues, they will be stilled; where there is knowledge, it will pass away. For we know in part and we prophesy in part, but when perfection comes, the imperfect disappears. When I was a child, I talked like a child, I thought like a child, I reasoned like a child. When I became a man, I put childish ways behind me. Now we see but a poor reflection as in a mirror; then we shall see face to face. Now I know in part; then I shall know fully, even as I am fully known. And now these three remain: faith, hope and love. But the greatest of these is love.

Alice quickly comments that there must be something here about groups.

She remembers doing endless grouping exercises in primary school; it was all about finding a common factor among the different things so that they could be correctly classified.

Ben can see that there are six things (they decide to refer to them all as gifts) and they form two groups. In the first group are prophecy, tongues and knowledge; in the second, faith, hope and love. The first group contains the charismatic revelatory gifts that they have now learned about. Alice says that, because of the context, knowledge here must mean the miraculous gift of knowledge Paul had written about in the previous chapter. The second group contains the more ordinary gifts: faith, hope and love. The first group was temporary; Paul said that those gifts would 'cease', 'be stilled' or 'pass away'. In contrast, 'these three remain'—that is, faith, hope and love.

They decide to draw up a table:

Temporary	Remaining
Prophecy	Faith
Tongues	Hope
Knowledge	Love

Ben says that he can now see why Tom directed them to this passage; Paul was clearly saying that the miraculous gifts, those transmitted by the apostles, were temporary. The big question now is, how temporary? And does this passage give the answer?

Alice suggests that they go back to the passage and see what is clear. 'Perfection' in verse 10 and 'face to face' in verse 12 she considers, without doubt, to refer to the return of Christ; that is what she has been taught. But Ben quickly points out that she is making the same mistake they made with Acts 8, when they had assumed that the passage was talking about baptism in the Spirit although the subject is never actually mentioned there.

What is clear to him is that the event described in verses 10 and 12 causes the gifts in the first group to cease. To make any sense of the passage and the grouping, this must mean that the second group carries on after that.

Alice accepts his point. If the first group finished at Christ's return, that is, at the end of the church age, the second group would have to finish after that; but the New Testament specifically tells us that faith and hope will not be in heaven, so they must cease at Christ's return ('Now faith is being sure of what we hope for and certain of what we do not see', Heb. 11:1; 'For in this hope we were saved. But hope that is seen is no hope at all. Who hopes for what he already has?', Rom. 8:24). Faith, hope and love are the great characteristics of the church age. They will 'remain' during that time. Prophecy, tongues and knowledge must finish before faith and hope cease at the end of the church age. If both groups finished together, the whole basis of the grouping, the contrast between the groups and therefore the thrust of the entire passage fall apart. Alice realizes that this does appear to rule out Christ's return as being the event to end prophecy, tongues and knowledge, but she is reluctant to give up something that she has always believed.

'What then,' Alice asks, 'do you think is meant by "perfection" in verse 10, and "face to face" in verse 12?' Ben decides that an early trip back to Tom is required.

Tom explains that a more literal translation of 'perfection' in verse 10 would be 'that [thing] which is complete'.[1] This, in turn, makes more sense of Paul's contrast; the complete thing is compared with the 'partial' thing, the gifts in the first group: 'For we know in part and we prophesy in part ...'

If this translation is given, the passage reads:

Love never fails. But where there are prophecies, they will cease; where there are tongues, they will be stilled; where there is knowledge, it will pass away. For we know in part and we prophesy in part, but when that which is complete comes, the incomplete disappears.

Ben asks what the complete thing is. Tom replies that it is the Bible; the Corinthians did not have a New Testament as we have. They relied on verbal reports of the apostles' teaching, and the teaching of the prophets whom the apostles had endorsed through the laying on of their hands.

Even Paul himself did not have 'all truth'—it was to the apostles collectively that Christ made that promise, not to any individual.[2]

Ben asks whether Tom is not cheating by changing the passage; he considers the Bible to be the inspired Word of God. Tom replies that the original Scripture was inspired, but not the translation, no matter how good it is. Sometimes you have to go back to the original. He points out that the King James Version, loved and trusted by millions, talks in this whole passage about 'faith, hope and charity'. There was pressure on the seventeenth-century translators to use the word 'charity' to imply that the passage was talking of a Christian's duty to do good works, thought by many (then and today) to be essential to a believer's salvation. Modern translations have rightly chosen the word 'love' instead. But in the King James Version, the word 'perfect' in verse 8 was well chosen by the translators because, as any etymological dictionary shows, the original meaning of 'perfect' was 'complete', 'complete in all its parts', 'finished'; in many modern dictionaries this is also the first listed definition.[3] So the retention of the word 'perfect' (or 'perfection') in many translations today is not technically wrong, but unfortunately, in contemporary English, the word tends to convey more the idea of being without fault than its original meaning (and its meaning in the original Greek) of a finished or complete thing, a thing that has come to maturity after a long gestation.

Tom suggests that they now look again at Alice's grouping with this understanding of the word perfection:

Love never fails. But where there are prophecies, they will cease; where there are tongues, they will be stilled; where there is knowledge, it will pass away …

And now these three remain: faith, hope and love. But the greatest of these is love.

He says that Alice has done well to see that 'knowledge', in this first group, is the miraculous gift of knowledge, not intellectual knowledge. Many commentators have not realized this and have consequently stumbled in their interpretation of 1 Corinthians 13—including the great John Calvin! So, Paul said that the first group was temporary, but the second group remains. The first group contains miraculous revelatory gifts; the second group contains ordinary faith gifts:

Temporary revelatory gifts	Remaining ordinary gifts
Prophecy	Faith
Tongues	Hope
Knowledge	Love

Paul said that the first group would cease when 'the complete thing' came, and, importantly for our purpose, he then went on to compare the first group, not with the second group, but with Scripture: the 'complete thing' that would cause the 'partial thing' to cease:

> For we know in part and we prophesy in part, but when perfection comes, the imperfect disappears. When I was a child, I talked like a child, I thought like a child, I reasoned like a child. When I became a man, I put childish ways behind me.

Temporary revelatory gifts	Scripture
Partial revelation	Complete revelation

Paul, in effect, describes the partial revelation as 'childish', but the complete revelation as manly. Tom explains that by 'childish', he did not mean that the charismatic gifts were 'silly'. They were childish in that they only revealed a partial truth. An eight-year-old child might accurately say that the Battle of Hastings took place in 1066, but it would be an unusual eight-year-old that could evaluate that battle's significance in Anglo-French relations over the following five hundred years! Prophecy, tongues and knowledge were a true revelation of the mind of God, but they were an incomplete revelation, and therefore considered to be immature when compared with the complete New Testament. The comparison Paul was making was between the 'childish' revelatory gifts transmitted by the apostles and the 'mature' Scripture to come. There was nothing wrong with prophecy and tongues, but they were only a partial revelation of God's mind.

Now we see but a poor reflection as in a mirror; then we shall see face to face. Now I know in part; then I shall know fully, even as I am fully known.

Paul continued to make the contrast, saying that the things contained in the first group were not very clear (a poor reflection), while the thing coming would be clear (we will know fully); so we now have:

Revelatory gifts	Scripture
Partial revelation	Complete revelation
Childish	Mature
Not clear	Clear

Tom points out that, with her interpretation, Alice would be comparing the revelation of prophecy, tongues and knowledge, a partial thing, with the Lord Jesus Christ. Tom says that you cannot compare things that are not comparable. Apples and pears do not go together. It is more logical to compare and contrast a partial thing with a complete thing. Furthermore, the Lord is not anywhere in Scripture described as a complete thing—complete, that is, after a long gestation.

Alice replies that, whether she accepts that or not, it does not solve the problem of 'face to face' in verse 12.

Tom agrees. He now suggests that they go back to the Old Testament. In Numbers, there is a similar comparison between a less clear thing and a clearer thing when specifically talking about the revelation of the mind of God, as Paul was in 1 Corinthians 13.

Listen to my words:
'When a prophet of the LORD is among you,
   I reveal myself to him in visions,
   I speak to him in dreams.
But this is not true of my servant Moses;
   he is faithful in all my house.
With him I speak face to face,
   clearly and not in riddles;

he sees the form of the LORD.
Why then were you not afraid
   to speak against my servant Moses?'
(Num. 12:6–8)

Here God was saying that he revealed his mind in visions, dreams and riddles to ordinary prophets, but to Moses he spoke clearly—'face to face'. The verses make exactly the same point Paul made, contrasting a less clear revelation of the mind of God with a clearer revelation of the mind of God. Paul would obviously have known this passage well. Surely, Tom suggests, Paul chose precisely the same phrase, 'face to face', deliberately, under the inspiration of the Holy Spirit ('For prophecy never had its origin in the will of man, but men spoke from God as they were carried along by the Holy Spirit', 2 Peter 1:21).

Furthermore, Tom asks Ben and Alice to consider the illustration Paul used to make his point about the less-clear nature of the first group of gifts compared with the clearer coming 'perfection'. Paul was saying that using the spiritual gifts was like looking in an unclear mirror that gives a poor reflection—or, as the King James Version memorably puts it, 'we see through a glass, darkly'. He went on to say that, in contrast, when you have a perfect mirror, you see 'face to face'.

'And whose face do you see in a mirror?' asks Tom.

'It is your own,' says Alice.

'Yes,' says Tom. 'You don't see somebody else, certainly not Christ. Paul was saying that you see there your own face clearly, and a clear mirror is obviously better than an unclear mirror for that purpose.'

Paul was using the mirror illustration to drive home his point. And what was his point? That the gifts in his first group were temporary because they were only 'in part', so they could not be a clear revelation of God's truth; they only told part of the story. They were going to be replaced with something clearer.

'If you had a new mirror in your bathroom that was much clearer than your old one,' says Tom, 'it would be unlikely that you would look in the unclear mirror again.'

Scripture is clearer because it is complete: it tells all of God's truth, not just bits and pieces. Tom points out that, when Paul said it was complete, he did not mean that it would tell us everything; rather, it would tell us everything we need to know to be the Christians God wants us to be: 'All Scripture is God-breathed and is useful for teaching, rebuking, correcting and training in righteousness, so that the man of God may be thoroughly equipped for every good work' (2 Tim. 3:16–17). In the King James Version, verse 17 reads: 'that the man of God may be perfect ...' Ben and Alice immediately realize that, again, the word 'perfect' must mean 'complete', 'mature'; no Christian is 'without fault'!

> Now we see but a poor reflection as in a mirror; then we shall see face to face. Now I know in part; then I shall know fully, even as I am fully known.

As Paul continues, Tom says, we realize that in this clear mirror we are not going to 'see' anything at all—at least, not in a literal sense. Instead, we are going to know something. Paul said that with this mirror, 'I shall know fully, even as I am fully known', so the mirror is all about knowledge! But we are not surprised by this because we realize that Paul is using the mirror as a metaphor for Scripture. Interestingly, if Paul were talking about the return of Christ, not Scripture, he could have clarified it now. The phrase we might have expected—'then I shall know all things'— could easily have been expressed in the Greek. Wayne Grudem, a theologian who does not accept that Paul was talking here about Scripture, admits that the phrase that Paul actually used expresses the much lesser concept of a 'fuller understanding'.[4]

But what precisely is this 'fuller understanding', this knowledge that is going to come? It is self-knowledge; we are going to see something about ourselves. Again, Grudem concedes that, in using the phrase 'I shall know fully, even as I am fully known', Paul was saying that, with this coming thing, his knowledge of himself would resemble God's knowledge of him.[5] Paul was here talking of the true self-knowledge that only the completed Scriptures could bring. In them we see the gospel in all its glory. We see that, even though in God's eyes we are sinners deserving only punishment, he covers all our sins by the blood of Christ. Scripture leads us (or, at least, all those whom the Spirit draws) to this self-knowledge. This is the very point that James made about the 'perfect law' (the Bible) in his letter, where he also used the same metaphor, describing Scripture as a mirror:

> Do not merely listen to the word, and so deceive yourselves. Do what it says. Anyone who listens to the word but does not do what it says is like a man who looks at his face in a mirror and, after looking at himself, goes away and immediately forgets what he looks like. But the man who looks intently into the perfect law that gives freedom, and continues to do this, not forgetting what he has heard, but doing it—he will be blessed in what he does. (James 1:22–25)

In this mirror, we 'see' (know) ourselves as we are: sinners before a holy God. We see what is wrong; we see what needs putting right. We should then do what the Bible tells us, and we will be blessed.

The writer to the Hebrews conveyed a similar message: 'For the word of God is living and active. Sharper than any double-edged sword, it penetrates even to dividing soul and spirit, joints and marrow; it judges the thoughts and attitudes of the heart' (Heb. 4:12).

So we have:

Revelatory gifts	Scripture
Partial revelation	Complete revelation
Immature	Mature
We see ourselves as in an unclear mirror	We see ourselves as in a clear mirror
We know in part	We know fully, as we are known by God

Ben asks why Paul didn't include any of the other miraculous spiritual gifts in his first group of gifts. Tom says that that is an interesting point; all the sign gifts seem to have been lost to the church when the Bible was completed and the last apostle died. Tom asks whether Ben and Alice have any thoughts as to why these other miraculous gifts were excluded from the list. Ben and Alice are stumped.

Then Ben says that he's got it: the gifts in that first group, while being different from one another, were all gifts that revealed the mind of God—even, as we have seen, the gift of tongues. Healing, the message of wisdom, special faith, miraculous powers and discerning spirits were really not the same sorts of gifts: they were not conveying truth; they were not prophetic in that strict sense. The point of Paul's comparison was between partial prophetic revelation (prophecy, tongues and knowledge) and a complete prophetic revelation (Scripture). If Paul had placed the other gifts in the first group, it would, as we have said, have been like comparing apples with pears. So the fact that those gifts were not included in that group was not an accident; it was to reinforce the point of Paul's comparison, which is all about prophetic knowledge, partial and complete.

Tom agrees. Paul was saying that the temporary revelatory gifts would give way to Scripture, leaving the enduring gifts of the church age: faith, hope and love.

Finally, Tom points out, in verse 13, Paul goes back to this second, 'remaining' group:

And now these three remain: faith, hope and love. But the greatest of these is love.

The whole of these two paragraphs, verses 8–13, is about the temporary nature of the spiritual gifts compared with the enduring gifts of the church age; but we might have forgotten Paul's opening statement—'Love never fails'—which he left hanging in the air. In verse 13, he came back to it and singled out love from this second group, calling it the greatest gift. Alice says that she knows why this is: it outlasts all the gifts, the temporary and the remaining, and it alone goes on into heaven.

'Yes,' says Tom, 'when we see Christ return in glory, when every knee will bow, faith and hope will fall away; then we will be with him for ever in his world of love. If you believe that "perfection" refers to the return of

Christ, this emphasis, Paul's different comparisons and the climax of the passage are all lost.'

Tom concludes by saying that, in chapters 12–14 of 1 Corinthians, Paul was addressing the issue of spiritual gifts: their dangers and blessings. It is the most sustained teaching on the miraculous gifts in the New Testament. Why did he devote so much time to this subject here? Because, it seems, the Corinthians were dazzled by these gifts. Paul told them not to be. And in chapter 13 he said why: because the miraculous gifts would 'cease'. In other words, they were temporary—that is, temporary compared, not with eternity, but with the abiding gifts of the church age.

If the argument was that these gifts were going to last throughout the church age along with faith, hope and love, what was the point Paul was making to the Corinthians? Paul's actual point was that the gifts the Corinthians were so wrapped up in were temporary, and he explained why: they were going to be replaced with the Bible.

Tom says that not only does the interpretation he has outlined mean that Paul's teaching is contextually appropriate, it also makes sense of Paul's argument and comparisons, and, what is more, it is consonant with the rules of Greek grammar.

Ben is listening carefully to all this and is at last convinced. He sees that the whole basis of the different comparisons Paul makes—between the temporary charismatic gifts and the abiding gifts of the church age; then between the temporary charismatic gifts and the completed Scripture—now makes sense. Despite what he first thought, he sees Tom's analysis to be a natural and 'unforced' interpretation. In fact, he cannot see how Alice's idea of it being all about the return of Christ can be made to fit at all, especially as this would mean that the second group of gifts would have to continue beyond the point of Christ's return into heaven. He asks Tom how the commentaries which hold Alice's view cope with this problem. Tom replies that, despite considering the passage and consulting commentaries on it for more than twenty-five years, he has never found one that can answer that difficulty.

Notes

1. The Greek word translated 'perfection' is *teleion*. See **Gerhard Kittel, Gerhard Friedrich** and **Geoffrey W. Bromiley** (eds.), *Theological Dictionary of the New Testament* (Grand Rapids, MI: Eerdmans, 1964); and **W. E. Vine,** *Vine's Expository Dictionary of New Testament Words* (McLean, VA: McDonald Publishing, n.d.).

2. For example, Peter not only did not know everything that Paul did, he also said that he did not always even understand it when Paul revealed it (2 Peter 3:16)! An argument can be made that when Paul used 'we' in 1 Corinthians 13, he was referring to the Apostles. See **Douglas Judisch,** *An Evaluation of Claims to the Charismatic Gifts* (Grand Rapids, MI: Baker, 1978), p. 49.

3. See **Walter W. Skeat,** *The Concise Dictionary of English Etymology* (Wordsworth Reference; Ware: Wordsworth Editions, 1993) p. 45; *The Cassell Dictionary of Word Histories* (London: Cassell, 1999); *The Oxford English Reference Dictionary* (Oxford: Oxford University Press, 2002); *The Chambers Dictionary* (Edinburgh: Chambers, 2003).

4. **Wayne Grudem,** *The Gift of Prophecy in the New Testament and Today* (Wheaton, IL: Crossway, 2000), p. 197.

5. Ibid.

12. A final revelation

In the past God spoke to our forefathers through the prophets at many times and in various ways, but in these last days he has spoken to us by his Son, whom he appointed heir of all things, and through whom he made the universe. (Heb. 1:1–2)

Ben and Alice come home from Tom's, reeling somewhat from all that they have had to absorb. The implications are clear. If the Bible contains God's final revelation to his people, then seeking further revelations, whether from impressions and feelings or through the miraculous spiritual gifts, is pointless; worse still, it is quite wrong. But after talking with some of her new friends, Alice still has questions in her mind. She and Ben decide that they need to meet with Tom again as soon as possible.

Alice tells Tom that several of her new friends have told her that it is impossible to be dogmatic: you cannot bind God. He will reveal himself in any way he chooses, whatever we think about 1 Corinthians 13.

Tom says that he knows that many do say this—often with the rider that, though God may choose to reveal himself today in a miraculous way, it will be 'only occasionally'. Tom challenges Ben and Alice to consider the fatal flaw of this viewpoint. Ben suggests that we must be able to bind God to some things, otherwise we would have no hope as Christians. Alice also sees the truth of this. She says that we can bind God to the fact that he will be true to his Word, that he will judge the living and the dead, that he will take all those to heaven who are united to him, that his promises will not fail, that he will not lie, that the church will not be lost … and so on!

'Precisely,' says Tom. 'The whole basis of the Christian hope is that we *can* bind God. We can bind God because God binds himself.'

And, Tom points out, those who add the rider 'but only occasionally' are, in effect, accepting the theology of ongoing miraculous gifts but denying them in practice—the worst of both worlds!

'Yes,' says Alice. 'In fact, it is they themselves who are binding God!'

Ben does not follow this logic. Tom says, 'I think I know what Alice is saying: nowhere in Scripture does God say that he will reveal himself by miraculous means "occasionally". Any person making such a qualification is, in effect, saying how he or she thinks God should reveal himself.

'In any case,' he continues, 'I have never seen such an assertion qualified by an explanation of what is meant by "occasionally". If a church has seventy members, and each has a miraculous revelation once in his or her lifetime, that church might have such a revelation every year. If there were fifty such churches in a city, there might be a revelation every week—and so on.'

'The issue then,' says Ben, 'is to establish whether God does bind himself to the way in which he is going to communicate with believers in the church age.'

'Yes,' says Tom, 'and where can the answer to that question be found?'

'In the Bible,' says Ben.

'But what I want,' says Alice, 'is more assurance that the Bible teaches that the gifts transmitted by the apostles will give way to a completed Bible. I want to see it taught clearly in Scripture, apart from in 1 Corinthians 13.'

Tom says that there are references in both the Old and New Testaments to the concept of prophetic revelation finishing. So Ben and Alice go away with some more Scripture references. They try to tackle them, but fall at the first hurdle with the Daniel passage Tom has given them.

Daniel

Seventy 'sevens' are decreed for your people and your holy city to finish transgression, to put an end to sin, to atone for wickedness, to bring in everlasting righteousness, to seal up vision and prophecy and to anoint the most holy.

Know and understand this: From the issuing of the decree to restore and rebuild Jerusalem until the Anointed One, the ruler, comes, there will be seven 'sevens', and sixty-two 'sevens'. It will be rebuilt with streets and a trench, but in times of trouble. After the sixty-two 'sevens', the Anointed One will be cut off and will have nothing. The people of the ruler who will come will destroy the city and the sanctuary. The end will come like a flood: War will continue until the end, and desolations have been decreed. He will confirm a covenant with many for one 'seven'. In the middle of the 'seven' he will put an end to sacrifice and offering. And on a wing of the temple he will set up an abomination that causes desolation, until the end that is decreed is poured out on him. (Dan. 9:24–27)

They go back to see Tom. He agrees that Daniel can be a difficult book, and says that there are various interpretations about the timing of the events spoken of. But he explains that a widely held and respected interpretation of this passage is that the 'seventy "sevens"' refer to the time span allotted to the Jerusalem that was rebuilt after the Babylonian exile, and that verses 26–27 refer to its destruction in AD 70. The promised Messiah did indeed come to the rebuilt city, in approximately AD 30, and he atoned for wickedness at Calvary. The destruction of AD 70 followed, and with it, the end of sacrifice and offering predicted in verse 27 ('In the middle of the "seven" he will put an end to sacrifice and offering').

But Tom says that what must be noted is that the events are linked with the sealing up of vision and prophecy ('to seal up vision and prophecy', v. 24). The years between AD 30 and AD 70 was the precise time when the words of the apostles were being recorded for us.

Daniel had correctly prophesied this climax of the prophetic age. The time the great prophet Moses had spoken of had come: 'The LORD your God will raise up for you a prophet like me from among your own brothers. You must listen to him' (Deut. 18:15).

'This,' Tom explains, 'was the prophet to end all prophets—the Lord Jesus Christ. God's revelation was complete.'

Zechariah

'On that day a fountain will be opened to the house of David and the inhabitants of Jerusalem, to cleanse them from sin and impurity.

'On that day, I will banish the names of the idols from the land, and they will be remembered no more,' declares the LORD Almighty. 'I will remove both the prophets and the spirit of impurity from the land. And if anyone still prophesies, his father and mother, to whom he was born, will say to him, "You must die, because you have told lies in the LORD's name." When he prophesies, his own parents will stab him.

'On that day every prophet will be ashamed of his prophetic vision. He will not put on a prophet's garment of hair in order to deceive. He will say, "I am not a prophet. I am a farmer; the land has been my livelihood since my youth." If someone asks him, "What are these wounds on your body?" he will answer, "The wounds I was given at the house of my friends."' (Zech. 13:1–6)

Ben asks, 'What day is this that is referred to?'

Tom replies that we have to be careful about being dogmatic in the interpretation of prophecy, but he (and many others) sees this as referring to the same period of time as referred to in the Daniel prophecy. The fountain is the fountain of Christ's blood shed on Calvary. This would be the beginning of the church age. It is apparent that, during that time, any prophecy would be a false prophecy. Why? We are forced to draw the conclusion that this is because prophecy has ended.

Ben and Alice decide that that is enough for one day, and leave to consider the New Testament passages by themselves.

Ephesians

Consequently, you are no longer foreigners and aliens, but fellow-

citizens with God's people and members of God's household, built on
the foundation of the apostles and prophets, with Christ Jesus himself
as the chief cornerstone. (Eph. 2:19–20)

Alice asks whether these are Old Testament prophets and New Testament
apostles, or apostles and prophets of the New Testament, or both. Ben says
that he thinks the first interpretation is the most likely, but in any case, the
point is made: God's household, the church, is built on the teachings of
these men duly recorded in Scripture. You cannot keep building a
foundation.

Hebrews

In the past God spoke to our forefathers through the prophets at
many times and in various ways, but in these last days he has spoken to
us by his Son, whom he appointed heir of all things, and through
whom he made the universe. (Heb. 1:1–2)

Alice can see that this teaches that something different had happened in
the church age, the 'last days', compared with the Old Testament era. But
what was that different thing? The passage seems to say that God's
revelation would not come by prophets, but by his Son. Ben points out to
Alice that the words of the Son are recorded in the Bible. In fact, the Son
is the very Word of God: 'In the beginning was the Word, and the Word
was with God, and the Word was God' (John 1:1). The apostles supervised
the recording in the New Testament of all that Jesus had taught them—
the 'all truth' into which their Pentecostal gifting had guided them (John
16:13).

... This salvation, which was first announced by the Lord, was
confirmed to us by those who heard him. God also testified to it by
signs, wonders and various miracles, and gifts of the Holy Spirit
distributed according to his will. (Heb. 2:3–4)

Ben considers it reasonable to assume that 'those who heard him' were the
apostles. The implication of this is that the miraculous spiritual gifts,

'distributed according to his will', that is, through the apostles, were given as temporary sign gifts to confirm that the apostles' teaching really was from Christ himself.

Jude

Beloved, when I gave all diligence to write unto you of the common salvation, it was needful for me to write unto you, and exhort you that ye should earnestly contend for the faith which was once delivered unto the saints. (Jude 3 (KJV))

Alice remembers that Ben mentioned this verse in an earlier study, but she can see that the full force of it comes across in the King James Version. She accepts that something that was once delivered cannot be added to.

Revelation

I warn everyone who hears the words of the prophecy of this book: If anyone adds anything to them, God will add to him the plagues described in this book. And if anyone takes words away from this book of prophecy, God will take away from him his share in the tree of life and in the holy city, which are described in this book. (Rev. 22:18–19)

At first, Ben thinks that these verses do not really address their subject. None of the Christians he and Alice have met at the charismatic church consider that any of their prophecies add to the Bible, which they believe to be complete. It is Alice who points out the anomaly: when those believers say that the Bible is complete, they must mean that it is a complete revelation. Any further revelation, whether added to the Bible or not, is still a further revelation. Ben says that he can see that; what is more, when the book of Revelation is studied, it becomes apparent that it contains prophecies that sweep majestically through mankind's history, referring back to the Garden of Eden and forwards to our future bliss in heaven. Any other prophecy is, by definition, adding to those prophecies. Surely the apostle John was saying that there would be no more prophecy.

Alice considers that it is no coincidence that the Bible, that complete revelation, closes with those very words. But when Alice asks one of her new friends from the charismatic church about this, her friend says that their modern-day prophecies are 'different' from those in the Bible, so they do not add to the completed Scripture. Neither Ben nor Alice knows what to make of this—so back to Tom's they go.

13. A certain revelation

And we have the word of the prophets made more certain, and you will do well to pay attention to it, as to a light shining in a dark place, until the day dawns and the morning star rises in your hearts. Above all, you must understand that no prophecy of Scripture came about by the prophet's own interpretation. For prophecy never had its origin in the will of man, but men spoke from God as they were carried along by the Holy Spirit. (2 Peter 1:19–21)

A new kind of prophecy?

Ben and Alice ask Tom about this concept of two kinds of prophecy. Tom explains that these Christians do not believe that they are adding to the Bible because they believe that their own prophecy is different from that contained in the Bible. Their prophecy, they would say, does not carry the same authority as biblical teaching; they would never say, 'Thus says the Lord'.

Tom says that Wayne Grudem is a prominent exponent of this view. He is a respected theologian and a charismatic Christian who has published several helpful books. The views he expresses in his book *The Gift of Prophecy in the New Testament and Today* are widely held by Christians of charismatic persuasion. Grudem makes the argument that the New Testament prophets are different from the Old Testament prophets in two ways.

Firstly, New Testament prophets could give prophecies that contained elements that were true or false. He says, 'Each prophecy might have both true and false statements in it, and those would be sifted and evaluated for what they were';[1] '... there is almost uniform testimony from all sections of the charismatic movement that prophecy is imperfect and impure, and will contain elements that are not to be obeyed or trusted.'[2]

Secondly, even when they were true, their prophecies did not have the same authority as those of their Old Testament counterparts. Grudem defines New Testament prophecy as '... speaking merely human words to report something God brings to mind'.[3]

We know that the New Testament prophets were commissioned by the apostles, whereas the Old Testament prophets (like the apostles) were commissioned directly by God, so in that sense, Tom says, he agrees with Grudem. But this does not necessarily imply that the New Testament prophets lacked authority or infallibility, even if that authority was subject to the apostles.

Tom further points out that Grudem's two points of necessity hang together. A redefinition of prophecy away from its Old Testament meaning is required if we are to allow prophets whose prophecies are 'imperfect and impure' to continue in the church. An Old Testament prophet whose prophecies contained 'both true and false statements' would come to a sticky end: 'But a prophet who presumes to speak in my name anything I have not commanded him to say, or a prophet who speaks in the name of other gods, must be put to death' (Deut. 18:20).

Grudem's definition of prophecy as being 'human words ... [that] God brings to mind' is very close to the careful use of Scripture and its wise application that any evangelical would commend. When we looked at prayer, we saw that a role of the Holy Spirit is to bring to mind Scripture and give us wisdom. We mentioned, for example, Colossians 1:9: 'For this reason, since the day we heard about you, we have not stopped praying for you and asking God to fill you with the knowledge of his will through all spiritual wisdom and understanding.' In other words, we can ask God to bring Scripture to our minds, and ask for wisdom in applying it, both in our own lives and in the counselling of others.

The difference with the approach of modern charismatic Christians is that they would hold that a Christian can have thoughts brought to mind by God that would go beyond Scripture. For example, imagine that a Christian man is having difficulty deciding whether or not to change his employment; a fellow Christian might say, 'I feel that God is telling me that it is his will that you leave that job.' We can see that this approach is very close to the traditional evangelical guidance teaching in which the reliance is on feelings and impressions.

The problem is that the Bible does not give a mechanism for evaluating these sorts of prophets or their prophecies. Somebody might say to you, 'I have a word from God: it is time to get married!', but, as Wayne Grudem readily concedes, this person might be right or wrong. Grudem quotes other charismatics who think that perhaps as few as one in ten claims to predictive prophecy might be correct.[4]

Tom thinks that the debate about the infallibility of the New Testament prophets will take them too far from their subject, but he recommends some books that Ben and Alice could look at.[5]

Alice says, 'We're talking about language again, aren't we? It's similar to what we learned about the call to ministry. I can see that it is quite different for somebody to come to you and say, "God is telling me it is time for you to marry", rather than saying, "I think it is wise for you to marry". One is a matter of truth—either God did say this, or he did not; the other is a matter of personal judgement.'

Tom agrees. Basically, this charismatic view teaches that somebody can give a word as being from God which could be right or wrong. Tom believes that, although the overwhelming majority of such Christians are totally sincere in their prophecies or 'words from God', they cannot get away from the fact that, in any other sphere, we would call somebody who told the truth sometimes but not always foolish, or worse. Yet a large section of the church is happy to say that this is how God speaks today.

The Christian life is often described as a battle, and the Christian's armour includes the Word of God: it is the Christian's sword; it is sharp, certain and true (Eph. 6:17; Heb. 4:12). In this analogy, a believer has one sword, not a selection, any of which might prove worthless. In the Christian life, we need clarity and certainty as to what God wants of us. Soldiers need to receive clear orders from their commanding officer. If on the battlefield they keep saying, 'I think our orders might be …', the battle is already lost.

A matter of authority

Ben asks Tom whether, despite these difficulties of application, he thinks modern charismatic believers are right in their belief that there are two types of prophecy, one authoritative, the other not. In other words, if it could be agreed that a believer really had a message from God, they nonetheless could treat that message simply as good advice because the message was not in the Bible.

Tom asks Ben what he thinks prophecy is. 'Speaking words from, or prompted by, God,' Ben replies. He continues: 'From what you say, it seems that many who believe in contemporary charismatic gifts would be happy with this definition; it is just that, if those words are not in the Bible, they think that they are not authoritative.'

'All right,' says Tom. 'But why are the words of the Bible authoritative?'

Ben replies, 'Because they are in the Bible!'

'No,' says Tom. 'The Bible does not lend God's words authority. It is the other way round: God's words give the Bible its authority. God's words have authority because they are God's words; there are not two different levels of authority attached to them. And it is worth pointing out that, if the Bible did give God's words recorded there a different (and greater) authority, the Bible itself would be a greater authority than God!'

Tom says that we know that Christ did, and must have said, many things that are not recorded in the New Testament: 'Jesus did many other things as well. If every one of them were written down, I suppose that even the whole world would not have room for the books that would be written' (John 21:25). But any of the other things he said must also have been true. They were all God's words. They were all authoritative. It appears that Paul wrote at least three letters to the Corinthians, yet only two survive; surely they also contained authoritative apostolic teaching. The fact that not all Christ's words, or all those of the apostle Paul, are in the Bible does not diminish the authority of them. In his wisdom, God decided that we did not need those teachings to live an effective Christian life. But we must believe that when God speaks, he speaks. Just because what he says is not in the Bible should not diminish its authority. If it is of God, it should be obeyed.

'So,' continues Tom, 'if somebody in your church says to you, for example, "God is telling me you should leave your employment", and that person is considered to be truthful, and if you accept the concept of continuing prophecy, you should obey this word as much as any biblical instruction.'

Alice says that she thinks that, if a person is just giving advice, he or she should say so and not couch it in the language that makes it seem to be a word from God, a prophecy or a word of knowledge. 'In any case,' she says, 'I am convinced, from what we have learned so far, that God has said in the Bible that he will not continue with prophecy of any sort in the church age.'

A matter of certainty

Tom says that one of the most momentous experiences of the apostle Peter's eventful life must have been on the Mount of Transfiguration. There he saw Moses and Elijah, and there Jesus Christ was 'transfigured' before his very eyes: 'After six days Jesus took with him Peter, James and John the brother of James, and led them up a high mountain by themselves. There he was transfigured before them. His face shone like the sun, and his clothes became as white as the light. Just then there appeared before them Moses and Elijah, talking with Jesus' (Matt. 17:1–3).

This episode is of great significance. All Jews would recognize that Moses represented the law and Elijah the prophets, the two together representing the whole Old Testament. But the voice from heaven said, 'This is my Son, whom I love; with him I am well pleased. Listen to him!' (v. 5).

In his second letter, when referring to that experience, Peter wrote this:

And we have the word of the prophets made more certain, and you will do well to pay attention to it, as to a light shining in a dark place, until the day dawns and the morning star rises in your hearts. Above all, you must understand that no prophecy of Scripture came about by the prophet's own interpretation. For prophecy never had its origin in the will of man, but men spoke from God as they were carried along by the Holy Spirit. (2 Peter 1:19–21)

There are differences of opinion as to what precisely Peter meant by the expression 'And we have the word of the prophets made more certain'. Peter was either comparing his Mount of Transfiguration experience with Scripture, Old and New; or 'Scripture' was the Old Testament, and he was saying that God was reaffirming that this Scripture pointed to Christ and his eventual return in glory.

Whichever it was, the point was made that Christ was the supreme revelation to which Scripture pointed. And, although he did not replace Moses and Elijah, Christ eclipsed them, for he was the one of whom they spoke.

It is in the very next verse (2:1) that Peter went on to say, 'But there were also false prophets ...' Peter was contrasting these false prophets with Scripture, which is certain, true and authoritative.

An illustration

Tom asks Ben and Alice to think of the church as a supermarket, one that stocks a great variety of food. Sixty-six different types of food sold there contain a cast-iron guarantee by an unimpeachable source that they are good for us; in fact, we are told by that source that they are all we need to grow healthy and strong (2 Tim. 3:16–17).

The supermarket also carries some other foods from a different manufacturer which cannot guarantee their purity; in fact, when pressed, this manufacturer admits that some of this food might actually be harmful for us, but it cannot categorically say which is which. What is more, our unimpeachable source has actually warned about using these other products: 'And if the [false] prophet is enticed to utter a prophecy, I the LORD have enticed that prophet, and I will stretch out my hand against him and destroy him from among my people Israel. They will bear their guilt—the prophet will be as guilty as the one who consults him' (Ezek. 14:9–10).

The manufacturer of these other foods sometimes claims that its products are from the same unimpeachable source; but we are told that it should be careful about doing that: 'You shall not misuse the name of the LORD your God, for the LORD will not hold anyone guiltless who misuses his name' (Exod. 20:7).

Ben and Alice say that they have already made their choice about which foods their family is going to consume.

Notes

1. Ibid., p. 61.
2. Ibid., p. 90.
3. Ibid., p. 63.
4. Ibid., p. 210.
5. See **David Aune,** *Prophecy in Early Christianity and the Ancient Mediterranean World* (Grand Rapids, MI: Eerdmans, 2002). **Budgen** (*The Charismatics and the Word of God*) and **Bloomfield** (*Guidance*) also mount convincing counter-arguments to Grudem's thesis, claiming that New Testament prophets did speak authoritatively. See particularly the Appendices in both books.

14. A sufficient revelation

All Scripture is God-breathed and is useful for teaching, rebuking, correcting and training in righteousness, so that the man of God may be thoroughly equipped for every good work. (2 Tim. 3:16–17)

Tom has invited Alice and Ben round to discuss another aspect of Scripture apart from its completeness, finality and certainty: its sufficiency. That Scripture is sufficient, he tells them, is really the essence of all that they have talked about.

He suggests that they look at some verses:

All Scripture is God-breathed and is useful for teaching, rebuking, correcting and training in righteousness, so that the man of God may be thoroughly equipped for every good work. (2 Tim. 3:16–17)

Alice says that this is an obvious one. Tom says, 'Yes it is, but let's not miss what Paul was saying.' He says that Paul was telling Timothy that Scripture is sufficient to make the man of God 'thoroughly equipped for every good work'. Paul did not say that Scripture is a good starting point. Scripture is sufficient to equip us for our entire Christian life. The Old Testament counterpart to this verse might be considered to be: 'The secret things belong to the LORD our God, but the things revealed belong to us and to our children for ever, that we may follow all the words of this law' (Deut. 29:29).

So Deuteronomy was saying that the law (the Bible) is there for us even though it does not tell us everything. Paul was saying to Timothy that Scripture was sufficient to make him the Christian God wanted him to be.

Tom asks Ben and Alice to consider what happened when Jesus was tempted by the devil in the wilderness.

'What did he do?' asks Tom.

Ben says that Jesus quoted from Scripture: 'The tempter came to him and said, "If you are the Son of God, tell these stones to become bread." Jesus answered, "It is written: 'Man does not live on bread alone, but on every word that comes from the mouth of God'"' (Matt. 4:3–4).

Alice points out that, if anybody could have countered the devil using his experience, it was the eternal Son of God. Paul tells us that 'though he was rich, yet for [our] sakes he became poor' (2 Cor. 8:9). Jesus had left all the glories of heaven to be born in a stable. But instead of speaking of this, he quoted the Bible! Tom agrees with Alice, and adds that Peter similarly reinforced the concept of the sufficiency of Scripture: 'His divine power has given us everything we need for life and godliness through our knowledge of him who called us by his own glory and goodness' (2 Peter 1:3). Although he does not specifically mention Scripture in this verse, we have seen that this is the chapter in which Peter refers to Christ's transfiguration and then goes on to emphasize the importance of Scripture.

Furthermore, the emphasis in Paul's pastoral letters is often an appeal to a defined body of teaching that he wanted Timothy and Titus to focus on. He talked of:

- sound doctrine (1 Tim. 1:10)
- the truth (1 Tim. 2:4)
- the deep truths of the faith (1 Tim. 3:9)
- the truths of the faith (1 Tim. 4:6)
- sound instruction (1 Tim. 6:3)
- the pattern of sound teaching (2 Tim. 1:13)
- the good deposit (2 Tim. 1:14)
- the word of truth (2 Tim. 2:15)
- the trustworthy message (Titus 1:9).

His specific instruction to Timothy was: 'Until I come, devote yourself to the public reading of Scripture, to preaching and to teaching (1 Tim. 4:13).

Ben says that this emphasis in Paul's letters on preaching and teaching does not make sense if the knowledge of God's will was going to be transmitted in a subjective or charismatic way in the church age. Why study to be a 'workman', as Paul exhorted Timothy to do (2 Tim. 2:15), if revelation would come in a vision or tongue?

'And,' says Tom, 'consider those twenty-one eldership qualifications we talked about earlier: no elder is required to have the gift of prophecy, or, indeed, any miraculous gift. A particularly striking omission is the gift of discerning spirits; if any miraculous gift were needed by the leadership in a church of ongoing supernatural revelation, it would be this one. Instead, Paul said that an elder needed to be able to teach—but teach what?'

Alice says it must be Scripture—that defined body of truth for the church age.

A key question

Tom says, 'Let me ask you a question.' He tells Ben and Alice to imagine that a non-Christian friend asked them what they believed, and they tried to express to their friend what it was to have a personal faith in Christ and to be born again of the Spirit. Ben and Alice would say, in summary, that they were Bible-believing Christians. If, in reply, their friend asked them what this meant, which of the following statements would they be most likely to use?

- I believe that the Bible contains God's Word.
- I believe that all of the Bible is God's Word.
- I believe that, today, only the Bible contains God's Word.

Ben says, 'I suppose it must be the last one. A Muslim and a Jew can agree to the first statement; a Roman Catholic, a Jehovah's Witness and a member of any number of different sects can agree the second; but only an evangelical Christian will agree with the last statement.'

'You're right,' says Tom. 'An evangelical believes that he or she is saved by grace alone, through faith alone, based on Christ's death on the cross alone. In contrast, these other faith systems say we need more: we need the teachings of their religious systems. How can we be sure we do not?'

'Because,' Ben says, 'the Bible tells us we do not. The Bible tells us all we need to know to be secure with Christ.'

Tom replies with an emphatic 'Yes! We believe these things because we believe that Scripture teaches us all we need to know to reach that heavenly shore safely. Being an evangelical is very much about accepting the sufficiency of Scripture.

'Evangelical Christians accept that the Bible alone is the guide for their life of faith. They will not accept any other claim to have authority over them in this life, unless the Bible itself gives the person that authority.'

'How do you mean?' asks Alice.

Tom explains that the Bible says that we are to obey all legitimate powers, including the state; so we have to accept, for example, that in the areas over which the state has control, we are to obey.

'But we do not have to obey a Roman Catholic priest or the Watchtower organization,' Tom continues. 'We do not depend on any of their systems for our eternal security, nor are we subject to any code of personal behaviour that they might teach; instead, we base everything on our Saviour and what he taught. This truth was bitterly fought over in the Reformation and we should not lightly throw it away; but that is a subject for another day.'

Tom asks Ben and Alice whether they can now see the danger in accepting a modern-day prophecy as being God's word or even a human word prompted by God, whether that prophecy comes from the present pope, the Watchtower Society or any prophet in a charismatic church, no matter how well intentioned the 'prophet' may be.

They can.

God's will found

15. Scripture applied

My son, if you accept my words
   and store up my commands within you,
turning your ear to wisdom
   and applying your heart to understanding,
and if you call out for insight
   and cry aloud for understanding,
and if you look for it as for silver
   and search for it as for hidden treasure,
then you will understand the fear of the LORD
   and find the knowledge of God.
For the LORD gives wisdom,
   and from his mouth come knowledge and understanding.
(Prov. 2:1–6)

The view that God is waiting for us to find the individual life plan he has for us is deeply ingrained in the theology of the Christian church today. Often the only difference among believers in this area is whether God is waiting for us to correctly interpret the subtle signs he is sending via our emotions or providential circumstances as he guides us towards the path he wants us to take, or whether he is going to reveal the path with a charismatic revelation—perhaps a prophecy, dream or vision. When doubt is cast about this way of looking at the Christian life, believers often express that they are at a loss as to how to move forward in their decision-making. They literally do not know what to do next.

But we have seen with Ben and Alice that the Bible really is sufficient for us to make each decision with a clear conscience. We can ask the Holy

Spirit for wisdom, and for help in recalling Scripture; we do not have to second-guess what God's mind is on a particular matter. Every decision can be submitted to God's Word, prayer and the counsel of others, as we see fit—whether it be a life-changing decision or one seemingly much less consequential. When believers have done this, when they have used this 'wisdom' approach, they can go forward in confidence, knowing that they have not in some way missed God's will for their lives, which is often a fear for those who believe in subjective guidance processes.

Let's come back to Ben and Alice for more practical examples, to see how, with the help of Tom, they use this wisdom approach in dealing with some more decisions that will certainly affect their lives.

Ben and Alice leave Africa

After several years in Africa, Ben and Alice go to see Tom for help with another decision. They tell him that the church they have planted has made good progress. Furthermore, a very promising young African man is being considered for the pastorate. Their own two children are coming to secondary-school age and there are no suitable schools for them in the area. Also, a new opportunity has arisen to serve in their home church. The question is, should they leave Africa and head for home?

Tom says, 'Let's start with what we know: the Bible is clear that everything we need to know to live a life that pleases God is contained there. We have seen that the Bible is our only reliable guide. What you have to do now is wisely apply those biblical principles.'

Ben says, 'I know what you're saying. We have our sure and certain Bible, but, on the other hand, we now have this particularly slippery decision to make; we do not want to do it on our own.'

Tom says, 'OK—let's go through it together.'

Firstly, he tells them, they are to serve God, seeking to use the gifts he has given them:

> We have different gifts, according to the grace given us. If a man's gift is prophesying, let him use it in proportion to his faith. If it is serving, let him serve; if it is teaching, let him teach; if it is encouraging, let him encourage; if it is contributing to the needs of others, let him give

generously; if it is leadership, let him govern diligently; if it is showing mercy, let him do it cheerfully. (Rom. 12:6)

Tom says that, between them, they believe that they possess gifts of leadership, teaching and encouragement. Those gifts have been put to good use in Africa, but circumstances are changing. What Ben and Alice are asking is whether it would now be best to use these gifts elsewhere. Tom says he believes that, because their church and the missionary society which facilitated their work did not accept them as missionaries based on a mystical call, it is not necessary for them to seek a further mystical call from God to return home. Instead, they can freely meet with all the parties involved, including representatives of the church in Africa, and decide the best course of action.

Many factors will have to be considered and different priorities weighed:

- The ability of the church in Africa to continue and thrive without them. The apostolic example seems to be to plant churches and move on once local leadership is in place; as Paul instructed Titus: 'The reason I left you in Crete was that you might straighten out what was left unfinished and appoint elders in every town, as I directed you' (Titus 1:5).
- The needs of their children: 'If anyone does not provide for his relatives, and especially for his immediate family, he has denied the faith and is worse than an unbeliever' (1 Tim. 5:8).
- Any opportunities for service back home using their recognized gifts. As we have seen in Romans 12, Paul exhorts us to use our gifts; he wrote to Timothy: 'Do not neglect your gift, which was given you through a prophetic message when the body of elders laid their hands on you' (1 Tim. 4:14).
- What they want to do: their own desires and wishes. As we have learned, this is a perfectly legitimate consideration: 'Now when I [Paul] went to Troas to preach the gospel of Christ and found that the Lord had opened a door for me, I still had no peace of mind, because I did not find my brother Titus there. So I said goodbye to them and went on to Macedonia' (2 Cor. 2:12–13).

'So,' concludes Tom, 'perhaps the next step is for you to ask God in prayer to help you recall the relevant Scriptures:"For this reason, since the day we heard about you, we have not stopped praying for you and asking God to fill you with the knowledge of his will through all spiritual wisdom and understanding" (Col. 1:9). And ask for wisdom in applying the principles involved:"If any of you lacks wisdom, he should ask God, who gives generously to all without finding fault, and it will be given to him" (James 1:5). Then seek counsel and wisdom from all the parties involved and mature Christian friends:"Plans fail for lack of counsel, but with many advisers they succeed" (Prov. 15:22).'

'That's what we're doing now,' remarks Alice.

'Yes,' says Tom, 'but still the decision will ultimately belong to you. You must look to see that what you decide is rooted in what you believe honours God and the cause of the gospel.'

Ben and Alice weigh what Tom has said, and, after praying and consulting others, decide to leave Africa and head for home. On their return, they are welcomed with a special church service. They have honourably served God and do not feel that they are in some way going against God's calling.

More decisions ...

Some time after returning home, Ben and Alice discover that their seventeen-year-old eldest daughter, Clare, despite her Christian profession, is pregnant, and the father of the child is not a Christian. How can they use their understanding of the Scriptures to steer a way ahead now?

They discuss it between themselves and realize that nobody is without sin; yet God has freely forgiven all those who belong to him. As their daughter certainly belongs to them, they decide to forgive her without reservation. But of course, as with any sin, there are consequences.

Should Clare bring up the child alone? Or should she be encouraged to marry the father of the child? The apostle Paul said, 'Do not be yoked together with unbelievers. For what do righteousness and wickedness have in common? Or what fellowship can light have with darkness?' (2 Cor. 6:14). But is this a binding instruction for all time in every circumstance? Alice and Ben consider not, because in 1 Corinthians 7, Paul said that, if you find yourself married to an unbeliever, you should not seek a divorce. Paul was presumably imagining a situation in which one partner had been converted after marriage, but, nonetheless, he did not instruct such a couple to separate. After discussing it with their church leadership, Ben and Alice decide to suggest to Clare that she marries the young man. Clare, however, is quite unwilling to do so!

As parents, they know from the New Testament that they can expect their children to be obedient (Eph. 6:1); but they also realize that the Ten Commandments speak of children 'honouring' their parents, the Bible recognizing that, as children grow into adulthood, there is a clear shift of responsibility in their duties. Where does Clare fit in here? The answer to this is dependent on Ben and Alice's particular family and the culture in which they live. They certainly do not want to antagonize their daughter: 'Fathers, do not embitter your children, or they will become discouraged' (Col. 3:21).

In light of all this, Ben and Alice decide that they have to treat Clare as an adult, and do not press her into a marriage she does not want. With this application of wisdom rather than seeking a 'revelation', Ben and Alice have escaped a trap. They have not said to Clare, 'We feel that the Lord is telling us that you should marry this man.' If they had, Clare would be disobeying her parents, and, if she stuck with her decision, she would be perceived by them to have disobeyed God.

An unspiritual approach?

As time has gone on, Ben and Alice have gained in standing in their local Christian community and have often shared their understanding of Scripture with a wider group of Christians. But some think that their wisdom approach to decision-making is unspiritual; it is believed that there is not enough emphasis on a believer's dependence on the Holy Spirit's indwelling and guidance. But Ben and Alice are clear: the Holy Spirit's role is to draw us to Christ, to encourage us in our Christian lives, to motivate us to serve Christ and to be a 'moral compass' pointing us towards a holy life. But the Bible never says that his role is to guide us towards an individual life plan.

Ben and Alice realize that, in contrast, contemporary evangelicalism
has developed a decision-making theology that is rather like using a
modern-day Urim and Thummin—only it is a complex machine with
various subjective inputs and often erratic outputs. In the absence of any
biblical model, or, indeed, instructions on how to use it, no two Christians
seem able to agree on how the thing actually works. Others say that
looking for different providences and inner impressions to guide us must
be right because it works! There often follows an anecdotal account in
which a (usually famous) Christian received an impression of a mystical
call and had a long ministry blessed by God. But Ben and Alice see that
God blesses Christians whenever they look to serve him, no matter by
which particular process that service came about. And, they point out, it
must be remembered that many people will have claimed a mystical call
and had disastrous ministries, but those are not the stories that are written
about.

A further problem occurs when, if Christians differ over a particular
issue, perhaps in a church meeting, the decision-making process is based
on extra-biblical revelations. How can there be such differences if,
especially after prayer, some have been 'led of the Lord' to a particular
conclusion? But Ben and Alice see that the New Testament clearly allows
for differences of opinion between believers, for example: 'One man
considers one day more sacred than another; another man considers
every day alike. Each one should be fully convinced in his own mind'
(Rom. 14:5). Paul was saying, 'Think the issue through and make up your
mind about it. But it will not necessarily be the same conclusion that
others come to.' Later in the same chapter, he wrote, 'So whatever you
believe about these things keep between yourself and God. Blessed is the
man who does not condemn himself by what he approves' (Rom. 14:22).
In other words, it might be wise sometimes to keep your differing
opinion to yourself!

Despite all of this, Ben and Alice realize that many Christians still prefer
to seek a 'word' or a 'feeling' that they can ascribe to God, and effectively
try to move responsibility for their decisions on to him. Such people are
worried that, if left to themselves, they will make a 'wrong' decision. Alice
says that she understands why this is, but Ben believes that there is no need

to fear. If the decision is made using biblical guidelines, there is no such thing as a wrong decision. If all reasonable steps have been taken, we can leave the outcome to God—even if that outcome proves at first sight to be unfavourable. God never promised us a life without pain or difficulty, yet we know that 'in all things God works for the good of those who love him, who have been called according to his purpose' (Rom. 8:28). Alice and Ben know that many feel safer maintaining the status quo until God 'tells' them to do something different. So, instead of taking the initiative in using their gifts to serve God, they wait for 'guidance'. This in turn leads Christians to criticize the wisdom approach, saying that, unless believers are 'called' to the mission field or other Christian work, none will go. But Ben and Alice believe that it is more likely to be the traditional guidance theology that is hindering God's work. Believers often have the gifts, opportunities and aptitudes, and really there is nothing to stop them serving God. But instead they are frozen into inaction, fearing that perhaps they will go 'in their own strength'.

Ben and Alice are confident that any Christian work is carried out in God's strength if God-honouring ways of going about it have been used. The call is not a mystical communication from God: the call is the need, the providential opportunities to serve, the gifting of the individuals and their motivation.

A Christian's responsibility ...

Ben and Alice see that a Christian's responsibility is to grow in the knowledge of, and obedience to, Scripture. They know that the wisdom approach they have embraced requires a Christian to have confidence in, and a growing understanding of, the Bible. It is no surprise, therefore, to find that the Bible itself commends this: 'Do your best to present yourself to God as one approved, a workman who does not need to be ashamed and who correctly handles the word of truth' (2 Tim. 2:15); 'Brethren, be not children in understanding: howbeit in malice be ye children, but in understanding be men' (1 Cor. 14:20, KJV). The writer to the Hebrews rebuked those who were not making such progress:

In fact, though by this time you ought to be teachers, you need someone to teach you the elementary truths of God's word all over again. You need milk, not solid food! Anyone who lives on milk, being still an infant, is not acquainted with the teaching about righteousness. But solid food is for the mature, who by constant use have trained themselves to distinguish good from evil. (Heb. 5:12–14)

Believers need to work at getting to know their Bibles, praying and asking God to bring Scripture to mind, asking for wisdom and consulting others. Then they should be bold and make their decisions, having the confidence to use biblical language to describe the process and not claiming extra-biblical revelations. They should go forward in faith and seek to undertake the work God has prepared beforehand for them to do (Eph. 2:10). The Holy Spirit will be with them to encourage and strengthen them, as he did the early church: 'Then the church throughout Judea, Galilee and Samaria enjoyed a time of peace. It was strengthened; and encouraged by the Holy Spirit, it grew in numbers, living in the fear of the Lord' (Acts 9:31). And, as Peter promised, 'If anyone speaks, he should do it as one speaking the very words of God. If anyone serves, he should do it with the strength God provides, so that in all things God may be praised through Jesus Christ. To him be the glory and the power for ever and ever. Amen' (1 Peter 4:11).

... And a Christian's freedom

At their next meeting with Tom, Ben and Alice share how much they now realize that the wisdom approach to decision-making means they have a responsibility not only to study Scripture, but also to take ownership of their Christian lives and their decisions. Tom adds that the wisdom approach gives enormous freedom as well. Ben says he knows this: they can serve God and live their lives as they choose, as long as they stick with biblical principles. Nobody can tell them what to do—or what not to do; they are free agents before God. Tom asks how he feels about this. Ben says, 'Marvellous!'

But Alice says that, although she realizes that Christian decision-making is so often arbitrarily based on feelings, impressions and casual providences rather than biblical principles, she nevertheless has sympathy with those who want assurance that God has specifically guided them, especially in their bigger decisions. Tom replies that it takes time for us to grow in confidence in this area. Paul wrote this about Epaphras: 'He is always wrestling in prayer for you, that you may stand firm in all the will of God, mature and fully assured' (Col. 4:12).

Epaphras was praying that the Colossians would be:

'... FIRM IN ALL THE WILL OF GOD'

Tom asks, 'Where is this will to be found?'

'In the Bible!' Ben and Alice reply in unison.

'... MATURE'

Tom asks, 'How do we achieve maturity in the Christian life?'

'By studying and putting into practice the teaching of Scripture,' says Alice. She adds that 2 Timothy 3:16 was her first memory verse in Bible class!

'... AND FULLY ASSURED'

'In other words,' Tom says, 'Epaphras was praying that we should be confident to stand firm on the Bible: to trust that, in the Bible, we find all the will of God.'

'Perhaps,' Tom continues, 'we should pray this same prayer for one another?'

'Always,' remarks Ben.

16. The greatest of these is love

This is how God showed his love among us: He sent his one and only Son into the world that we might live through him. This is love: not that we loved God, but that he loved us and sent his Son as an atoning sacrifice for our sins. (1 John 4:9–10)

The church is in a muddle over its guidance teaching; that is certain. However, the church of God runs on wheels of confusion, and always has done, so we should not despair. God will work his purposes out through each of us—and, sometimes, despite each of us.

But let us not finish without reminding ourselves that God is love. And despite the false prophecies that many from within the charismatic movement acknowledge to be an intrinsic part of their practice of the gifts; despite the fact that the subjectivity of traditional evangelical guidance teaching can give rise to a misuse of God's name; despite all our wilfulness in the face of the plain teaching of the Bible; despite our woeful ignorance of much of Scripture; despite all our misunderstandings, lack of zeal, and lack of love for him and for one another; despite all this, God still loves us.

Why? Because God is love. As the apostle Paul explained, when all the gifts have ceased, love will remain. It is the greatest of all the gifts; it will never fail. Heaven is a world of never-ending love. What love is this!

In the knowledge of that love, let us not wait for a mystical message or providential sign, but rather have confidence in the promises recorded in the Bible and go forward, using our God-given gifts and abilities to make our lives count for him.

Appendix: Some objections considered

He must hold firmly to the trustworthy message as it has been taught, so that he can encourage others by sound doctrine and refute those who oppose it. (Titus 1:9)

You cannot deny my experience

'I was fearful of preaching and I prayed much about it. Then God gave me assurance and courage and I have not had a problem with it since. It was God showing me his will that I should be a preacher. That's my experience—you cannot deny it.'

There is no problem with this experience at all. It was an answer to prayer. And this man is correct: no one can deny his experience. It is in the interpretation of the experience that the problem lies. I do not believe that, as evangelicals, we can say from this man's experience that God has told him to be a preacher.

'I had a dream that my workplace was going to catch fire the next day. I felt that God was warning me, so I did not go to work. The next day my office was destroyed by the flames. That's my experience ...'

As we have seen, there is such a thing as a casual providence. There are millions of Christians who will be having millions of dreams, and some, simply by chance, will be true. I actually had a very similar experience. When I was a schoolchild, I dreamt that my school burned down. I told my mother about it at breakfast, and that day, the school was extensively

damaged in a fire. This was before I was a Christian. In the end, an
evangelical has to put his or her trust in Scripture, not experience.

What about John 10:26–27?

> … you do not believe because you are not my sheep. My sheep listen
> to my voice; I know them, and they follow me.

The context of John 10 makes it clear that this verse is about the doctrine
of election. Those who belong to Christ—those who were chosen 'in
him before the creation of the world' (Eph. 1:4)—will respond at some
stage to the gospel call, because they are his 'sheep'. Unbelievers do not
respond because they are not his sheep. Those chosen by God will 'hear'
Christ's voice and come to him. The passage is not teaching that
Christians literally hear the voice of Christ any more than it is referring
to literal sheep.

Joel's prophecy, referred to in Acts 2, makes it clear that prophecy was for all the church age

> Then Peter stood up with the Eleven, raised his voice and addressed
> the crowd: 'Fellow Jews and all of you who live in Jerusalem, let me
> explain this to you; listen carefully to what I say. These men are not
> drunk, as you suppose. It's only nine in the morning! No, this is what
> was spoken by the prophet Joel:

> "In the last days, God says,
>   I will pour out my Spirit on all people.
> Your sons and daughters will prophesy,
>   your young men will see visions,
>   your old men will dream dreams.
> Even on my servants, both men and women,
>   I will pour out my Spirit in those days,
>   and they will prophesy.
> I will show wonders in the heaven above
>   and signs on the earth below,
>   blood and fire and billows of smoke.

The sun will be turned to darkness
    and the moon to blood
    before the coming of the great and glorious day of the Lord ..."'
(Acts 2:14–20)

Many believers of charismatic persuasion say that, by quoting this
prophecy of Joel, Peter was saying that the prophetic gifts would last
throughout the church age. But if we look carefully, Peter says in verse 16,
'this is what was spoken [of]', referring to the apostles speaking in
tongues. Even if the passage meant that the outpouring of prophecy
would be more widespread than the apostolic Pentecost, its fulfilment
could be in the story of the early church; certainly, this prophecy does not
require the gift of prophecy to continue throughout the last days for its
fulfilment. Furthermore, Scripture rarely expects a literal fulfilment of
many of these Old Testament prophecies concerning the 'day of the
LORD', especially those couched in such terms as 'smoke', 'blood' and so
on.

What about I Corinthians 1:7?
Therefore you do not lack any spiritual gift as you eagerly wait for
our Lord Jesus Christ to be revealed.

Some suggest that this verse implies that the gifts will be for the whole
church age, until Christ returns. The Corinthians were indeed waiting
for the return of Christ, as we are; but the verse does not say that Paul
expected the gifts to last throughout this period, just as he did not imply
that the Corinthians would be alive throughout that period. Incidentally,
the ubiquity of the gifts at Corinth is understandable—Paul spent
eighteen months there (Acts 18:11), during which time, he wrote, his
preaching was accompanied with a 'demonstration of the Spirit's power'
(1 Cor. 2:4–5).

I just cannot believe your explanation of I Corinthians 13
Paul advised Timothy to 'Do your best to present yourself to God as one
approved, a workman who does not need to be ashamed and who

correctly handles the word of truth' (2 Tim. 2:15). Christians can
honourably differ in their opinions about what Scripture teaches, but
Paul was saying here that we should do our homework and have a clear
reason for holding to one particular view. We should not simply say, 'I do
not accept your interpretation' and leave it at that, even if an alternative
interpretation can be credibly held. With this passage, however, it is not a
matter of picking one interpretation among several. What is the basis of
Paul's classification of the six gifts? One group 'passes away'; one group
'remains'. The second group must outlast the first group; but we have seen
that the second group cannot last into heaven. So the first group finishes
before heaven, and, for the contrast to make sense, the implication is that it
finishes a long time before. This is the whole basis of the classification, and
of the passage. Was Paul mistaken? Those commentaries that are thorough
in the exposition of the passage—taking into account the actual Greek
words and its grammatical construction—usually admit the difficulties in
making the 'perfection' in the passage refer to the return of Christ, but
then rarely offer another interpretation.

What about 1 Corinthians 14:39?

> Therefore, my brothers, be eager to prophesy, and do not forbid
> speaking in tongues.

At first, it does appear from this that Paul wanted tongues to continue. But
Paul was writing to the Corinthian church. Once the church had the
Bible, the revelatory gifts fell away—when they had the 'word of the
prophets made more certain', as Peter says (2 Peter 1:19).

Why is all this teaching about charismatic gifts in the New Testament if it was only for the first 100 years of the church?

The foundation of the New Testament rests on the apostles, so it is
important for us to know the basis of their authority. In light of this, it is
not surprising that a large section of the book of Acts is about the original
apostles and their ministry—hence the title of the book, 'The Acts of the
Apostles'. Although informative and useful for doctrine, it is not

necessarily all applicable today. The signs and wonders carried out by the apostles and passed on to others in fulfilment of Joel's prophecy attested to their authority. The miraculous revelatory gifts transmitted by the apostles enabled the rapid spread of the gospel across the known world while the New Testament was being written. It must be remembered that the early church was not a cohesive community as Israel had been, when all in that nation could gather to hear the Scriptures read or receive a new prophecy. The early church was a persecuted, multilingual, widely scattered minority.

If you exclude Acts, there is very little in the New Testament about the miraculous spiritual gifts at all—1 Corinthians 12 and 14 containing most of the teaching. And it is only the miraculous 'sign' gifts that have ceased; all the many other spiritual gifts remain, including faith, hope, and, of course, love.

Where do the tongues and prophecies come from if they are not genuine?

Jesus warned that there would be false prophecies, even from professing Christians:

> Not everyone who says to me, 'Lord, Lord,' will enter the kingdom of heaven, but only he who does the will of my Father who is in heaven. Many will say to me on that day, 'Lord, Lord, did we not prophesy in your name, and in your name drive out demons and perform many miracles?' Then I will tell them plainly, 'I never knew you. Away from me, you evildoers!' (Matt. 7:21–23).

In a sense, any confusion of the truth is demonic in origin, in that Satan is the 'father of lies' (John 8:44). When Peter tried to deny the truth of what Jesus had said, Jesus told him to 'Get behind me, Satan!' (Matt. 16:23). But in the passage above, Jesus was not saying that these false prophecies are demonic, but rather that they are 'evil', in that they confuse people about what is true.

It is possible sincerely to believe that God is speaking through you and yet be mistaken. Christians of charismatic persuasion accept that mistakes can be made; even in the best-taught, Scripture-based charismatic fellowship, not everything is automatically accepted as being from God. As we saw in Chapter 13, Wayne Grudem says that some prophecies are 'false'.

The signs and wonders of the modern-day charismatic movement prove it to be of God

Signs and wonders did indeed authenticate Old Testament prophets and New Testament apostles and prophets. But if you accept that these sign gifts were to cease with the apostles, as the various passages considered here suggest, you would expect the New Testament to begin to warn against signs and wonders. And we see that it does just that, Christ himself giving the first warning: 'For false Christs and false prophets will appear and perform great signs and miracles to deceive even the elect—if that were possible' (Matt. 24:24). And as the New Testament progresses: 'The coming of the lawless one will be in accordance with the work of Satan displayed in all kinds of counterfeit miracles, signs and wonders' (2 Thes. 2:9). In the last book of the Bible, signs and wonders are the very mark of the demonic activity:

> And he performed great and miraculous signs, even causing fire to come down from heaven to earth in full view of men. Because of the signs he was given power to do on behalf of the first beast, he deceived the inhabitants of the earth. He ordered them to set up an image in honour of the beast who was wounded by the sword and yet lived. (Rev. 13:13–14)

I cannot believe that all these good people are wrong

As evangelical Christians, we all have to face up to the fact that we are in a small minority, as Jesus predicted we would be. Sincerity has never been a test of truth. Many people sincerely hold views that are wrong. Millions of Muslims believe that Muhammad's dream, the basis of their faith, came from God; a Christian does not. We should respect the beliefs of others and their right to hold them, but this does not make their beliefs true. Many adherents of religions outside the orthodox Christian faith believe in further revelation; today in the Church of Jesus Christ of Latter Day Saints, for example, prophets play a key role in the leadership.

You appear to be a Sandemanian

A Sandemanian holds that simple mental assent to Christian teaching makes a person a Christian; a conversion experience and a personal love of Christ are not necessary. Theologians consider there to be three different sorts of faith: noticia, assensus, fiducia. Perhaps the following illustration will help explain how they differ.

In a remote part of Africa, no members of the local tribe had ever seen an aeroplane, or even heard that there was such a thing. When the concept was explained, they all absorbed the information (noticia) and some accepted that what was said was true (assensus). Somewhat remarkably, the following week, a small plane landed on a nearby field. But when the pilot offered the members of the tribe a ride, only one accepted (fiducia).

Only one member of the tribe put his trust in the plane. Similarly, only those who fully trust Christ are Christians. The most erudite university professor of biblical theology might not be a Christian—and, indeed, might not even claim to be one. Christians are born from above; their spirits witness with the Holy Spirit that they are the sons of God. They come to love and know the Saviour revealed in Scripture. A true Christian has an experiential life of faith; but this is not the same as saying that such a person receives messages from Christ about particular decisions that have to be made. I think we have seen that the Bible does not teach this.

What about I John 4:2–3?

This is how you can recognise the Spirit of God: Every spirit that acknowledges that Jesus Christ has come in the flesh is from God, but every spirit that does not acknowledge Jesus is not from God. This is the spirit of the antichrist, which you have heard is coming and even now is already in the world.

The argument here is that any charismatic manifestation that glorifies Christ must be from God. But it is clear from elsewhere in Scripture that, when someone speaks well of Christ, it does not necessarily authenticate that person; for example: 'When he arrived at the other side in the region of the Gadarenes, two demon-possessed men coming from the tombs met him. They were so violent that no one could pass that way. 'What do you want with us, Son of God?' they shouted. 'Have you come here to torture us before the appointed time?' (Matt. 8:28–29). So John's test obviously cannot be taken in isolation.

What about Matthew 7:15–20?

Watch out for false prophets. They come to you in sheep's clothing, but inwardly they are ferocious wolves. By their fruit you will recognise them. Do people pick grapes from thornbushes, or figs from thistles? Likewise every good tree bears good fruit, but a bad tree bears bad fruit. A good tree cannot bear bad fruit, and a bad tree cannot bear good fruit. Every tree that does not bear good fruit is cut down and thrown into the fire. Thus, by their fruit you will recognise them.

Some consider these verses to teach that, if people have a good standing in the Christian community, we should recognize them as prophets if they claim to be prophets. But Scripture makes it plain in many places that the possession of prophetic gifts does not correlate in any way to a person's state of grace. Judas Iscariot, it seems, performed all the miraculous gifts common to the other disciples (Matt. 10:1–8). The Corinthians, whom Paul castigated for their worldliness, came behind in no gift (1 Cor. 1:7; 11:17–23). Even Balaam's donkey managed to speak a word from God (Num. 22:28–30). The fruit by which a prophet is to be tested is his doctrine, not his deeds. A false prophet eventually teaches something untrue or makes a false prediction (Deut. 18:20–22). Some would say that any prophecy without miraculous authentication is, by definition, false.[1]

Notes

1   See **Judisch**, *Evaluation of Claims*, p. 21.

Books that support this thesis

SCRIPTURE ALONE IS OUR GUIDE

Bloomfield, Peter, *Guidance* (Darlington: Evangelical Press, 2006)

Friesen, Garry, *Decision Making and the Will of God* (Portland, OR: Multnomah, 1980)

Gilley, Gary, *Is That You, Lord?* (Darlington: Evangelical Press, 2007)

Jensen, Phillip, and Payne, Tony, *Guidance and the Voice of God* (Sydney: Matthias Media, 1997)

Meadors, Gary, *Decision Making God's Way* (Grand Rapids, MI: Baker, 2003)

THE MIRACULOUS REVELATORY GIFTS HAVE CEASED

Budgen, Victor, *The Charismatics and the Word of God* (Darlington: Evangelical Press, 1989)

Gromacki, Robert, *The Modern Tongues Movement* (Grand Rapids, MI: Baker, 1972)

Judisch, Douglas, *An Evaluation of Claims to the Charismatic Gifts* (Grand Rapids, MI: Baker, 1978)

Thompson, Jim, *Prophecy Today* (Darlington: Evangelical Press, 2008)

Warfield, B. B., *Counterfeit Miracles* (1918; reprinted London: Banner of Truth, 1972)

Books that present another viewpoint

SCRIPTURE AND 'GOD'S LEADING' ARE OUR GUIDE

Masters, Peter, *Steps for Guidance* (London: Wakeman, 1995, revised edition 2008)

THE MIRACULOUS REVELATORY GIFTS CONTINUE

Grudem, Wayne, *The Gift of Prophecy in the New Testament and Today* (Wheaton, IL: Crossway, 2000)